NROSS.

First Floor

Closet

Dreſſing Room

Garden Hall

Drawing Room

Dreſſing Room

Private Din: Room

Vestible

Dining Room

Charter Room

Second Floor

Drawing Room

Dining Room.

Closet

Sallen

Building a Nation *The Story of Scotland's Architecture*

RANALD MACINNES
MILES GLENDINNING
AONGHUS MACKECHNIE

Building a Nation

The Story of Scotland's Architecture

CANONGATE

First published 1999
by Canongate Books Limited
14 High Street, Edinburgh EH1 1TE
Text © Ranald MacInnes, Miles
Glendinning, Aonghus MacKechnie, 1999
Foreword © Kirsty Wark, 1999

ISBN 0 86241 830 5

This book is an abridgement of
A History of Scottish Architecture by Miles
Glendinning, Ranald MacInnes and
Aonghus MacKechnie, published by
Edinburgh University Press in 1996

The publishers acknowledge subsidy from the
Scottish Arts Council towards the publication
of this volume

Designed by Dalrymple
Typeset in Trinité and Myriad
Printed and bound in Italy
by Manfrini R. Arti Grafiche
Vallagarin spa

Frontispiece: Rosemount Viaduct,
Aberdeen, c.1950

Contents

Acknowledgements

This book provides a brief introduction to the highlights of five centuries of architecture in Scotland. It is an abridged version of our earlier textbook, *A History of Scottish Architecture,* published in 1996 by Edinburgh University Press. Readers seeking a full academic account should consult that book, which also includes a dictionary-style list of the principal works of Scottish architects. The present volume is intended to highlight key designers and trends in a more racy and simplified style. The work of editing, abridgement and picture research specifically for this shortened version was carried out by Ranald MacInnes: in recognition of his sterling efforts his name appears first in the list of authors. But we all take responsibility for the contents!

We would like to thank the following people, who helped us in various ways in the preparation of this book: Belinda Arthur, Iain Beckett, Gail Birnie, Ian Campbell, Stella Capaldi, Alan Clements, Brian Cole, T. F. Connolly, Richard Crotch, Richard Emerson, Ian Gow, John Hume, Juliet Kinchin, John Lowrey, James McCafferty, Alistair MacDonald, Allan MacInnes, Charles McKean, Katrina McPherson, Robyn Marsack, Sara Newman, John Paton, Paul Pillath, Veronica Steele, Margaret Stewart, Sally Stewart, Paul Stirton, Jane Thomas, David Walker, Kirsty Wark, Mark Watson, and Diane Watters. In addition, thanks are also due to the many other people who helped us during the three-year period of researching and writing *A History of Scottish Architecture;* their assistance has, of course, been a vital foundation for the present book.

Foreword

A major reassessment of our country's past is underway, including its
architectural culture. This rediscovery of Scotland's architectural history is affecting not only how we think of the past, but how we will
build for the future. The *Macmillan Encyclopedia of Architects* identifies
Scotland as the eighth biggest 'producer' of architects in the world.
Robert Adam, Alexander Thomson, Charles Rennie Mackintosh and
Robert Matthew are world figures, but only the famous few. There are
many other architects and engineers who deserve our attention. But in
the television series and in the book, we also wanted to focus on the
patrons of architecture and the historical circumstances which led
them to build in the way that they did.

We wanted to look at architecture in Scotland in its national and
international context through the people who *demanded* it, who created it. It is a huge story and we have had to be selective. This is not an
inventory. The subjects covered include the Stewart triumphalism of
Stirling, Linlithgow and Falkland; the New Town of Edinburgh in the
context of the Scottish appetite for planning; the astonishing story of
municipal Glasgow's 'can-do' culture of renewal; Romanticism and
Traditionalism from Bryce to Anderson, Lorimer and Charles Rennie
Mackintosh; urban 'regeneration' from Patrick Geddes to Page & Park;
the twentieth-century architecture of progress and modernity and the
reaction of Postmodernism, Conservation and Heritage.

None of the arts tells a story like architecture. Buildings are put up
by people, for people: kings and councillors, merchants, burgesses,
entrepreneurs, artists and tenants. Architecture is a three-dimensional
map of what we are. It is important that we understand and enjoy our
built heritage. But it is also vitally important that we expand on it by
building and planning well for the future. I can think of no better guide
than Ranald MacInnes, totally committed to Scotland's architectural
excellence, who brings his knowledge and passion to this story.

KIRSTY WARK

[1] Gardner Street, Partick,
Glasgow (built from the 1880s)

Introduction

What I want to do here is to look at the whole story, but especially to examine the evidence for a *Scottish* architecture, for this is the one question that has been asked over and over again since the beginning of our period. What is Scottish architecture? People have desperately sought buildings that will somehow stand for the idea of Scotland as a nation.

As Scotland approaches the Millennium there is much to look forward to – a new start, a new hope for the future. As so often, that hope will undoubtedly focus on a building: Scotland's new parliament. For centuries, buildings have been used to send out messages of power, comfort, wealth and even grief and despair. People have clamoured to have their voices heard in the designing of the new parliament: where it should be, what it should look like. We live in a democracy where everyone has the right to a say about new buildings. But it was not always so.

As people design and construct buildings they are making physical the ideas and aspirations of the society in which they live. And by looking at different stages of history, we can find out what people wanted from their buildings, their towns and their cities. We can tell a lot about our own attitudes, our politics and our sense of identity from the buildings being designed and erected now, here in Scotland. These buildings can help to define ourselves – to each other and to the rest of the world.

The establishment of a Scottish parliament is the single most important event in the history of Scotland for at least three hundred years. It has the possibility of making a difference to the lives of the people of Scotland. The building that houses it is therefore hugely significant, but perhaps less significant than the steps that parliament will take to encourage architecture and environmental planning to flourish. In order that people may feel empowered to play an active part in the governing of their country, the parliament building has to send out the right message to the people of Scotland.

Whatever Scotland's future may be, the new parliament is being established at a time of increasing globalisation. But we will discover as we look at Scotland's architecture that the flow of ideas between countries is not a recent phenomenon. Over the centuries, Scotland's designers have been influenced by the architecture of ancient Greece, Rome, England, France and Italy, and have adapted these foreign ideas to suit the needs of Scottish society. This is as true now as it has always been. The traffic of architects, and the inspiration behind their buildings, crosses national boundaries. But what – apart from location – makes a building Scottish? As a starting point, most people would recognise the use of stone and the uniform scale of building. In Scotland, there was plenty of good building stone. But how did this influence the monumental forms of Scottish buildings? For centuries this was an architecture of great mass, resembling at first the architecture of the Mediterranean rather more than that of northern Europe. There was no lack of building freestone in some other north European countries with very different architectural traditions of Gothic slenderness, such as France or England. So why use stone so consistently and with such commitment to uniformity?

A great street of tenements [1] is as recognisably Scottish as a Baronial castle but what – if any – ideas link these two types of building? And what happens when local stone is replaced with steel, glass and concrete? Can these buildings be said to belong to Scottish culture at all? Perhaps one of the most significant indications of how buildings tell the story of a nation's development is who is actually commissioning them. In the case of Scotland's parliament, it is the elected government, but if we look back through history the situation was very different.

The churches, the abbeys and the monasteries were built to glorify God and to act as power centres of the religious orders. But after 1450 – when our story begins – the focus of architecture dramatically shifted from the church to the monarchy, and from international Gothic to a new, recognisably 'national' style, promoted by the state. And the state was the Stewarts, the all-powerful Stewart dynasty. Secure in the comparative peace of its own 'imperial' realm, the Stewart kings embarked on an astonishing building campaign from the later fifteenth century. It involved the building and remodelling of some of the show-piece palaces and hunting lodges; even their spectacular 'holiday house' at Rothesay, which took Stewart power into the heart of the forfeited Lordship of the Isles.

The Stewarts' buildings were all massive, richly decorated and stone-built. But stone was at first for use on only the highest prestige dwellings, expressing nobility, power and, of course, permanence. Nowadays we take huge buildings for granted: the great icons of commerce and industry dwarf even the most grandiose of the Stewarts' fantastic creations. But if we are fully to appreciate the magnificence of these buildings we have to place them in the context of sixteenth-century Scotland. Previously, only the churches had been capable of making such bold architectural statements, and indeed the first signs of a 'return' to the heavier, more distinctively Scottish forms of buildings can be seen in church architecture. This is not surprising since the fifteenth-century clergy were the intelligentsia of their time: they were bound to be in the vanguard of any new cultural movement.

Scotland's search for an architectural identity was, of course, a sub-plot of this new 'nationalist' imperative. The main story is the country's general insistence on a separate identifiable culture: real, imagined and constructed. In literature, the Stewart historians – the clerics and the poets – constructed a nation myth that placed the monarchy in an unbroken line from Fergus MacFerquhard in 330 BC, descended from a Greek prince, Gathelus, and Scota, daughter of an Egyptian pharaoh. The arts were put to a nation-building use and so was architecture.

However, buildings had also to be useful in a practical sense and immediately we can see the central issue at the heart of the subject, the relationship between continuity and modernity in building construction and the attachment to the old that Charles Rennie Mackintosh called 'this instinctive affection which is so difficult to reason upon'. We will see that this insistence on cultural continuity and respect for the past has wavered: from the extremes of the Stewart dynasty with its books 'eftir owr ane Scottis use' to the consciously 'North British' phase of 'Elizabethan' architecture, and back onto a militant, imperial Scottish track with the full-blown rhetoric of the National War Memorial at Edinburgh Castle [2]. What is clear is that we cannot set architecture apart from the culture that produces it.

We might also ask at the outset: 'What separates architecture from building?' In this book, I am concerned with architecture designed by architects, but who were these architects? Over the course of the five-hundred-year period we see a gradual expansion of Scottish architecture, from the Stewart kings and a few nobles in the sixteenth century, to the twentieth century's involvement of diverse social classes as designers,

[2] Sir Robert Lorimer: Scottish National War Memorial, Edinburgh (1924–7)

patrons, or both. The present day professional with her qualifications and indemnities and armies of specialist consultants is very far removed from the sixteenth-century designer. Architecture was initially very much the 'property' of the monarch and, later, the court. However, as society changed, so did the range of buildings: from palaces to urban churches, schools, universities, tolbooth, then prisons, hospitals, even new towns. As Scottish society 'modernised' in the eighteenth century, the professional architect began finally to emerge, probably earlier in Scotland than elsewhere [3].

Finally, we might ask, what do we mean by 'Scotland'? Here we have no problem. Unlike many European countries, Scotland's borders have been settled, if ravaged, for centuries. The question of what Scottish architecture consists in is much more difficult. Must it look completely unlike any other country's to be claimed as Scottish? Prior to 1500 the story of Scotland's architecture was mostly concerned with pre-Reformation churches, closely allied to a mainstream European Romanesque – the round-arched style inherited from Roman imperial architecture – then Gothic, the slender, pointed style developed in twelfth-century France. In general, Scottish churches and religious houses were more monumental, more solid than their European counterparts, if much smaller in scale. They were also often more 'military' in character, occasionally, as Sir Walter Scott described Glasgow Cathedral [134], 'gloomy and massive'. Both Kelso [colour plate 1] and St Andrew's Cathedral have an unmistakable, castle-like quality which is nevertheless Gothic. Then, there was a sudden, breathtakingly jarring break from mainstream Europe. There began an extraordinary revival of the heavy forms and archaic mouldings of Romanesque architecture and this is where we begin, at St Machar's Cathedral, Aberdeen [4].

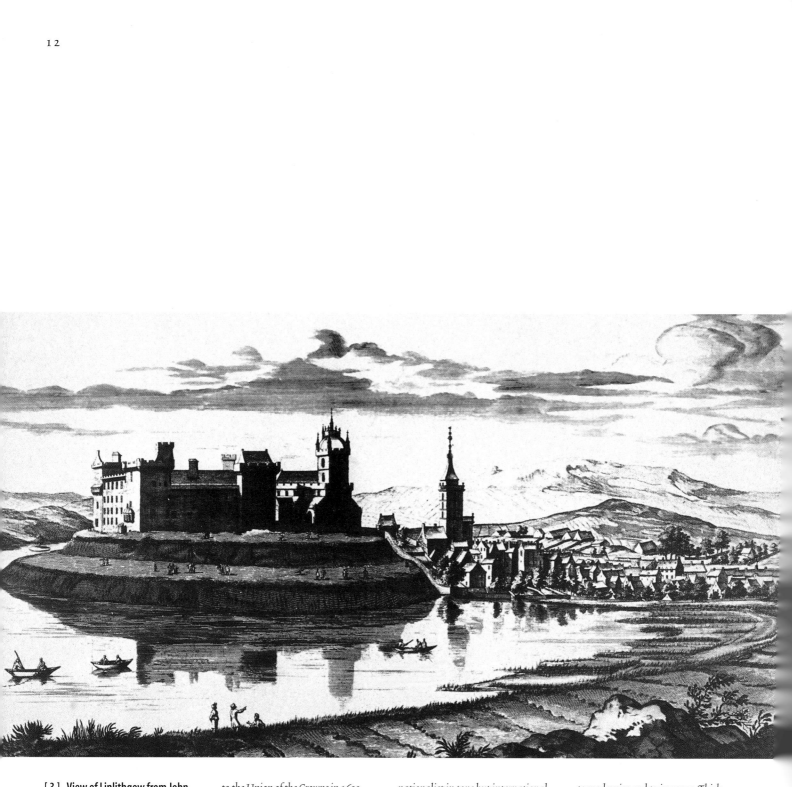

[3] View of Linlithgow from John Slezer's *Theatrum Scotiae* (1693)

Other nations have self-consciously sought their own identity, but few have been quite so concerned with the issue as Scotland. The reasons for this are largely political: Stewart nation and empire building in the fifteenth and sixteenth centuries, and the constant bugbear of assumed English overlordship throughout the period up to the Union of the Crowns in 1603. These two cultural factors produced an astonishing stone monumental architecture, intensely romantic in itself and later romanticised and revived time and again. Paradoxically, the new drive for Scottishness in culture was paralleled by a new openness to continental architecture. Thus was made possible great architectural hybrids which were nationalist in tone but internationalist in form. Linlithgow (above) has recently been identified as the sister building of a Renaissance quadrangular palace. James V's palace block at Stirling has long been closely associated with French architecture of the period. Scottish architecture has been caught in a great wheel of romanticism and revival but it has also been driven powerfully forward by the urge to modernise and to improve. Thirlestane Castle, for example, with its abundance of rippling towers and Baronial profile, was also fitted out for the Countess of Dysart by Sir William Bruce in the 1670s with the brand new invention of sash and case windows and WCs. A double balustraded wall walk on the scale of pavements was added, spectacularly modernising and enlarging a tower-house tradition.

THE STATE OF THE NATION

By the middle of the fifteenth century, the Stewarts had emerged victorious from their power struggles with competing nobles. We tend to take for granted the 'birthright' of the monarch, but this was not the case in fifteenth-century Europe, where claims to kingship had to be backed up by actions. James II's personal execution of the powerful head of the Douglas family in 1455 was such an action. Pretenders to greatness, like Douglas, among the Scottish nobility were finally dealt with. Apart from the Regent Albany's Doune Castle of 1419–24 (confiscated by James I in 1424), the Stewarts came to monopolise building as they used architecture in the creation of their new nation state. Equally important, the Stewarts' rule was accepted and endorsed by the papacy, to whom the monarchy continued to make overtures throughout the period up to the Reformation in 1560. This new cosmopolitan kingship of the Stewarts had to be appropriately housed.

In spite of the improved status and power of the Stewarts, however, the economic condition of the country was still very poor, and it is important to stress that the grandiose buildings of the monarchy in the fifteenth and sixteenth centuries were not the result of great royal wealth. Rather, they were the defiant gestures of an assertive monarchy, determined to play its part on the European diplomatic stage. Links with France were particularly close, but there was also a remarkable cultural connection with Italy, which led directly to the creation of the most important architectural set-piece, Linlithgow Palace [3]. Later, however, allegiances shifted. In the early and mid-sixteenth century Scotland suffered serious military defeats, including two at the hands of the English (Flodden, 1513; Pinkie, 1547). Following these, the nobility took diplomatic sides, during which the pro-French faction gradually lost out to the pro-English. Ultimately, religious pressures were pushing Scotland and England closer together, pressed home by the earlier intermarriage of the royal houses of the two countries.

The psychology of the Stewart mind is complex. Like many nations in this period, Scotland needed a past as much as it needed a future: a history that could be shown to have been free of foreign domination. We should bear in mind that the medieval world was not conceived as a 'society' in the modern sense, but as a strict hierarchy, with God at the top, and power cascading downwards through His earthly agent, the pope. At the heart of the Stewart sense of insecurity, therefore, was the claim of England as superior in a hierarchy. And we must remember that this was no technicality: the implications of overlordship were immense. In a 'devolved' kingship, the final arbiter, indeed the 'owner' of the title to lands in Scotland would have been the English crown. Of course, the Wars of Independence had been won, but the English claim continued, and had to be addressed.

A full-scale intellectual onslaught on the claim of English overlordship was made by Scottish historians. At first, clerics John of Fordun (c.1320–c.1384), Walter Bower (c.1385–1449), and Hector Boece (c.1465–1536) contested these claims by tracing a line of rulers back to Scota, the daughter of an Egyptian pharaoh. Over these thousands of years, they argued, Scotland had never been conquered, and a range of invaders, including the Romans, had been repelled. Among other things, this allowed for a celebration of the 'golden age' of Scottish 'fredome' during the time of the MacMalcolm dynasty (1058–1286), an era followed by the 'dark ages' of war with England. Against this background, a definition of national community and kingship gradually evolved, moving away from its origins in chivalry and religious duty towards a broader idea of the 'state' as we might now understand the term. Aberdeen was a powerhouse of this new historical, but more 'people-centred' approach, and in 1505 Hector Boece was chosen to head the new university there, King's College.

SCOTLAND AND THE RENAISSANCE

The Renaissance was not, of course, a single event, but a linked series of cultural tendencies, often full of apparent contradictions. In architecture, the Renaissance signalled the end of a medieval system of building based on Gothic architecture which had developed a soaring, 'pointed' aesthetic from the middle of the twelfth century to its 'Flamboyant' climax in sixteenth-century France and England. Gothic had itself developed out of Romanesque architecture, a round-arched or 'Norman style', developed from Roman imperial architecture. The eventual importance of the Renaissance was its 'redis-

covery' of what were believed to be eternal truths about the ancient world, particularly concerning proportion and the 'orders' of architecture – that is, the classical arrangement of columns and related elements. These were truths supposedly known to the Ancients and suppressed by the Goths. The definition of architecture today has broadened to include all aspects of construction, but at this time, and until relatively recently, architecture as a system was concerned purely with the classical orders, which could be applied to buildings almost superficially. An 'architect' was at first someone well-versed in the classical orders.

The story of Scottish Renaissance architecture is, therefore, one of a dynamic tension between this new, 'universal art' of architecture and the particular cultural requirements of building: between the cosmopolitan and the national. An Italian Renaissance palazzo is by no means a pure evocation of Roman antiquity, but rather a building particular to its time and place, and the same is true of buildings in Scotland to which Renaissance ornament or planning is applied. Nevertheless, the similarity between the prestige buildings of Scotland and Italy in the later fifteenth and early sixteenth centuries is striking.

Historians in every field have debated the meaning of the term 'Renaissance', but for architecture most discussions have centred on chronology. When, exactly, did the Renaissance begin? It is not an historical 'event', but a 'movement', discernible only long afterwards. Recently, and in line with revisionist historical writing, architectural historians in Scotland have sought to bring Scotland's Renaissance forward: out of the late-medieval and into the modern period. In most cases, the dating of buildings has not changed, but their significance has been reinterpreted. The grounds for this reassessment have been based on research by two scholars, Aonghus MacKechnie and Ian Campbell. But of all places, we might ask, why should Scotland, a relatively poor country on the edge of Europe, take up this advanced architectural tendency so enthusiastically and at such an early date? Let us look at the evidence.

[4]   West front of St Machar's Cathedral, Aberdeen

Drawn by R.W. Billings, 'The Baronial and Ecclesiastical Antiquities of Scotland'
1845-52. (The original towers were later altered to the form we see here.)

THE RENAISSANCE AND THE CHURCH

Scotland and England supported opposite 'sides' in the Great Schism of 1378–1417, which established rival papacies in Avignon and Rome. This encouraged the separation of the Scottish and English churches, a process already underway since the twelfth century. Scotland's support gave her a special place in Rome's heart, and good reason to develop an even stronger cultural connection. After 1417 there was a steady traffic between Rome and Scotland, her 'special daughter'. In 1453 alone, 47 Scots and 197 attendants were granted safe conduct for journeys to Rome, and there were many visits to Scotland by eminent Italian clerics, including the future Pope Pius II. This cultural interaction – mixed with a new, confident and 'independent' church – was bound to be expressed through architecture.

Scotland's first architectural steps towards the Renaissance were taken, as in Italy, when buildings assumed the form of low, massive structures, prominently featuring round arches and columns and archaic dog-tooth mouldings. Like the Tuscan revival preceding the Italian Renaissance, this may have been a conscious revival of the Romanesque architecture of the MacMalcolm 'golden age'. The revival of the architecture of this period took place in the centres of patriotic historical research: Dunkeld, St Andrews, Dunfermline and, most spectacularly, Aberdeen. In the third quarter of the fourteenth century, when Fordun was writing his chronicle as a chantry priest at Aberdeen, the first and most monumental set-piece of the style was begun: the nave of St Machar's Cathedral. Its stocky, round columns and massive west façade [4], round-arched doorway and line of seven slender, round-arched windows were flanked by heavy, warlike towers with crow-stepped gabled-cap houses.

THE RENAISSANCE AND THE STATE

The revival of MacMalcolm Romanesque was thereafter transformed into a more comprehensive Renaissance architecture, now focused on the 'imperial' rhetoric of the Stewart kings. The driving force here was an expanding conception of Stewart royal authority, based on the kingly origin-myth. In their new, relatively secure state, the Stewart monarchs were able to look to the development of their own culture. They became

[5] Roslin Chapel, Midlothian (from 1446)

Among many other examples of a 'classicising' tendency in the ecclesiastical architecture of the period, William Sinclair's Roslin Chapel included a range of unusual 'classical' features: heavily lintelled aisle bays suggesting a square, 'rationalising' tendency and a 'coffered' ceiling split into square compartments. In other cases it was the plan form – the rationalised, simplified or geometrical arrangement – which was intended to suggest classicism. We should bear in mind here that these experiments in 'rationalised' planning were echoing Italian Renaissance – and therefore Roman Catholic – practice. At James IV's own foundation at Ladykirk (c.1500; Nicholas Jackson, mason) or the collegiate chapel at Tullibardine (1446–1500) a cruciform centralised plan, in line with the contemporary plan for the Mother Church, St Peter's in Rome, was adopted. Centralised, 'rational' planning should not, therefore, be uniquely associated with the Reformation. A pattern found in many classical rural churches of the 17th and 18th centuries – a rectangular box with square headed windows and symmetrical front gable – was presaged at the Roman Catholic collegiate chapel of Innerpeffray (1506–7) and adopted as an exemplar of a plain Protestant preaching box. Clearly, the church had played a major part in introducing Renaissance forms and planning in Scotland, but now the focus of patronage was moving away from the church and towards the state, and from church buildings themselves to royal palaces.

[6] King's College, Aberdeen (1500–9)

At the other end of the 15th century, the chapel (1500–9) of Bishop Elphinstone's new King's College featured a prominent round-arched window and a corner tower with imperial crown steeple, later to become an architectural symbol of Scottishness (the Gothic Revival west front, on the right, was built in 1832). Clearly, the search was on for a style that could recall the past within the context of a modernising present. Within late-15th-century church architecture as a whole, 'Romanesque' architectural features began to appear in otherwise Gothic buildings. The clearest example of this

phenomenon is the round columns of the nave of Stirling's Holy Rude church (1450s–70s) a church which also included a detail dating possibly from James IV's marriage to Margaret Tudor in 1503. This was an archway, leading to the (later demolished) St Mary's Aisle, decorated with thistles and roses. So as the Stewarts looked back to the time before invasion from the South, paradoxically they also looked forward to a pan-British Stewart monarchy. The 'idea' of Scotland, having been expressed through the church, was now beginning to rest with the monarchy for its definition and development.

increasingly self-regarding and eager to express their power and status through diplomacy, dynastic marriages – and architecture. What appealed to the Stewarts was their own vision of Roman imperial power and authority, as opposed to the later humanism of the sixteenth century, developed in line with an interest in Renaissance 'citizenship'. Strangely for us today, along with this interest in antiquity and Ancient Rome came a fascination with the more recent 'Gothic' past of medieval courts and chivalry. This strand of Stewart ideology of course meshed neatly – through the cult of the court of King Arthur – with their claim to a 'revived' pan-British kingship. As usual, the Stewarts looked backwards to justify the way forward. But this hankering after medieval kingly duty and chivalry was to lead to the chivalric death of its greatest exponent – James IV [7] – at Flodden.

Now, of course, in order to produce what we regard as 'correct' classical architecture, James might simply have employed Italian architects. After all, he had imported other artists and musicians. Instead of importing a style, however, James presided over the creation of a classicising architecture which recalled the past, but created a suitably grandiose setting for the monarchy of the present.

[7] James IV (1473–1513)

James IV was determinedly a Renaissance prince: a 'humane prince', patron of musicians, poets and founder of the country's first printing press; a courtly prince, who loved hunting and martial display; a statesman, raising the profile of Scotland on the international stage. Most of James's efforts were directed towards Italy. He spoke Italian and employed Italian musicians, artists and craftsmen. He received gifts from three successive popes, and two of his sons, Alexander

and Robert, studied at Padua under Erasmus in 1507–8. James's Italophilia, and his fascination with the imagery of chivalry were dramatically expressed in a campaign of palace-building, designed to provide the appropriate setting for the ambitious Stewart monarchy.

THE STEWART PALACES

The shift in patronage from the church to the monarchy in the middle of the fifteenth century can be seen as the beginning of a slow process of 'filtering down' of the art of architecture, from the monarch's palaces eventually to the people's houses. But this final step was a very long way off. For the moment, architecture was the property of the crown and the higher nobility. Having taken control of architecture completely, the Stewarts built in a hurry and simultaneously at all their palaces in their undisputed power base of the Central Belt, spreading their monumental house style across their territory. These dramatic architectural symbols were planned and built once the whole kingdom of Scotland had been effectively brought under the control of the Stewart crown. James III, with 'ful jurisdictioune and fre impire within his realme' began the headlong drive to modernity and reconstruction based on the new power of a centralised 'state'. But for all their wealth, swagger and sophistication, the Stewarts laid the foundations of their building programme firmly in the past, stressing the continuity of their dynasty. Linlithgow, Edinburgh, Holyrood, Stirling, Falkland and Dunfermline were all extended from existing buildings. And this was a hugely expensive and complicated exercise, for which armies of workers and craftsmen were required. In the first half of the sixteenth century, Scotland experienced a 50 per cent rise in its population. The hauling and heaving required in the construction of these mighty palaces was carried out by cheap labour, to be finished by craftsmen from Scotland, Italy and France.

LINLITHGOW

Linlithgow [3] was first reconstructed by James I under Master of Works John de Waltoun in 1425–37, and was referred to as a 'palace' from 1429 – the first use of this description in Scotland. The word 'palatium' related originally to the official residence of the imperial Roman Emperor on the Palatine Hill and it is likely that the use of the word at this time consciously reflects the notion of the king as 'emperor'. Of all the palaces, the showpiece was undoubtedly Linlithgow. When James V's second French bride, Mary of Guise, saw Linlithgow's suave Italian Renaissance imagery – this great square fortress of culture and sophistication – she was impressed. The new queen declared it to be as magnificent as any French château. This was, of course, the effect that the palace was designed to have: to impress the neighbours, France and England, and to deliver a message of triumphalism and legitimacy to the Scottish nobility.

Of the present complex at Linlithgow, the east quarter (range) and parts of the north and south quarters were built at this time. During the reign of James III (1460–88) the south quarter was continued, ending in a square tower, and the west quarter was begun. Now the religious connections with Italy were beginning to bear secular fruit. As pointed out by Ian Campbell, the form of James III's and James IV's Linlithgow closely conformed to the most fashionable pattern of Italian palaces of the fifteenth and early sixteenth centuries, with its combination of symmetry and neo-chivalric imagery. This type of Italian palace was a direct descendant of the 'castro-praetorio' of imperial Rome, found for example at Diocletian's Palace at Split in Croatia, a building that was itself to become the focus of Robert Adam's architectural researches 250 years later.

Linlithgow was passed down from father to son, each of the kings adding to and developing it. But it was James III who first gave Linlithgow its Italian Renaissance character. Ian Campbell has proposed the true identity of the palace as a fantastic Scots–Italian creation. It seems likely that Italian masons were working in Scotland in the fifteenth century, but there was a more direct link with Italy, made through Anselm Adornes who was a merchant from Bruges of Italian descent. He made an extensive voyage to Italy and Jerusalem with his son in 1470, and presented an account of this journey to James III. In 1477 Adornes moved to Scotland and was made keeper of Linlithgow Palace. In Adornes's account, several Italian palaces of the Linlithgow type are favourably remarked on; for instance, the Castello Visconteo at Pavia is described as a 'very beautiful and large castle, square with a great tower at each side and a park behind', which would be a fair enough description of Linlithgow. Today, of course, we see the palace in a ruined, if expertly conserved, condition. The palace was burned by English soldiers of the Duke of Cumberland's army in 1746, and so much of the sophistication of the architectural composition has to be imagined.

The stone detailing and sculptural work at Linlithgow was merely a framework for the real artistry – that of the painters, who also belonged to the Incorporation of Wrights and Builders. An exuberant scheme of painted decoration was implemented in James V's time, including decorative glass and wrought iron, and striking colour schemes. The window surrounds were painted orange, and the harling (render coating) was brightly tinted. The harling which covered the palaces' rubble stone construction, and contrasted with the areas of expensive ashlar, has fallen off, and the external colouring (including profuse gilding and coloured paintwork) has vanished [colour plate 2].

It was the reign of James IV which saw the climax of Linlithgow's elaborate building programme. Princes used various means to express their status and their right to rule: the most potent of these means was undoubtedly architecture, which James IV practised almost to the point of recklessness. At Linlithgow, his most grandiose work was the rebuilding of the great hall or 'Lyon Chalmer'. Below this, was the main entrance passageway, fronted by massive chivalric towers: to the north, a new chapel with a range of round-headed windows in the manner of St Machar's. Internally, James created a brilliant suite of private and public rooms, fitting the status of the monarch. Here, we see for the first time sequences of internal spaces organised according to their architectural functions. This is the beginning of so-called state rooms – processional, formal spaces – taken up in the seventeenth-century great houses of the nobility. Linlithgow now took on the appearance of an Italian palace, as James completed the complex planned by his father. It was seemingly James IV who added the remaining three corner towers. The great hall was made far more grandiose, with new windows including a huge east window to light the royal dais, a range of large rectangular windows lighting a clerestory, and round-headed windows of Florentine Renaissance character to the inner courtyard. Elsewhere, an imposing sequence of apartments was formed in the south and west quarters, including a full-height range of galleries overlooking the courtyard.

Architecture and Politics

Architecture had the power to deliver the Stewarts' political message. James IV commemorated every significant event through the medium of architecture. When the English marriage took place, the princess ceremonially arrived in Edinburgh. A contemporary account records that 'at the entering of the … town was made a gate of wood painted, with two tourelles and a window in the midst. In the which tourelles was at the windows revested angels singing joyously for the coming of so noble a lady, and at the said middle window was likewise an angel, presenting the keys to the King and Queen.'

The son of James's dynastic marriage to Margaret Tudor was to be a new King Arthur, a Stewart ruling over the whole island. But that was a hundred years away. With the death of James IV on the battlefield of Flodden, the infant James V became king. On coming of age, James V began to build in typical Stewart fashion, first at Holyrood, which was more and more becoming the favoured royal residence and centre of government. At Holyrood, James V built the present north-west tower in the form of a Stirling Forework-like block [8] with turrets at all four corners, and containing vertically stacked apartments on each of the two upper floors. In 1535–6, in contrast to the martial symbolism of the towered block, a west range of apartments was added. The tall windows and glazed oriels recalled the contemporary palaces of Tudor England. As a complete set-piece, Holyrood was nothing less than a great, romantic palace, turreted and ostentatiously 'defended' with ornamental gun loops.

We should beware of reading too much into the much-vaunted French influence on Falkland [9] and Stirling. These are buildings that have no direct prototype unlike, for example, Bothwell's Crichton Castle. Comparisons have been made between the Palace block at Stirling and certain French buildings, but few architectural historians would accept Stirling as particularly 'French'. As usual, the Stewart court had kept its eye on the past while building for the future in a cosmopolitan, exceptionally up-to-date style. That style reflected, but did not mirror, the new political reality of the day, alliance with France. At Stirling, beyond the multi-towered walls of his father's triumphal arch, James V had created one of the gems of Scottish architecture, the Palace block and, to be sure, a very

[8] **A reconstruction of the Forework at Stirling Castle (c.1600)**
At Stirling, the scale of James's IV's architectural works was equally ambitious. The courtyard complex was again fronted by towers: a permanent gateway in the form of a triumphal arch, constructed of finely-worked ashlar (dressed stone). Inside the courtyard lay the Great Hall, fitted up and gorgeously finished in celebration of the royal wedding. Among the accounts of 1501 for work in preparation for the event are bills for 'scarlate' silk and 'welwous' (velvet) hangings and in 1503 for

'verdeouris [tapestry with rural scenes] bocht for hyngingis of galloryis and stares'. Italian embroiderers involved included the Florentines Simon and Francis Nicholai, much of whose work was done in gold thread. At the time of its construction, the Great Hall was the most spectacular secular space in these islands. But as grandiose as the Stirling complex was by the time of James IV's death in 1513, it was not until the reign of his son, James V, that the final phase was created.

[9] **South range façade of Falkland Palace, Falkland, Fife (c.1537)**

James V's work at Holyrood was the first of his building projects, but the last of the romantic Stewart set-pieces – for the time being. Architecturally and politically, the new king was looking in a different direction: towards France. James's marriage in 1537 to François I's eldest daughter, followed (after her death) by Marie, daughter of the Duc de Guise, was accompanied by a sudden change of architectural direction. Before his first marriage, James had travelled in France with a French mason, Mogin Martin. Later, the Duc de Guise sent two further masons from France. James's bride, Marie de Guise, was famously taken with Linlithgow, but in the future, its warlike symbolism was not to be employed. Falkland Palace, like Doune, came into the possession of the Stewarts through forfeiture. It was built up, again around a courtyard, as a hunting lodge, fronted by the usual badge of Stewart triumphalism, a massive round-towered forework in the manner of Stirling. However the courtyard was given greater architectural embellishment with work that is more 'classical', in the sense that the floors of the new ranges were expressed through the use of applied columns.

sudden shift to mainstream classicism had taken place. But the whole composition is crowned with crow-stepped gables, architectural emblems of Scotland even up to the present day. So the Palace block can be seen as a kind of monument to the Auld Alliance of France and Scotland, an architectural marriage of convenience.

COURT AND BURGH IN THE STEWART PERIOD

At first, non-royal works did not dare match the magnificence of the Stewart palaces. Any major works tended to pay homage to Linlithgow or another of the palaces. At Edzell [**colour plate 5**], Melgund and Carnasserie, the square, tower-and-hall form of Linlithgow was picked up. The nineteenth-century scholars of Scottish architecture, MacGibbon and Ross, were intrigued by the date of Melgund and Carnasserie and commented that they must have been 'built in imitation of the castles of an earlier period'. What seems likely is that they were built in imitation of Linlithgow, which only gradually assumed its square shape. However, many of the houses of the higher nobility and clergy during this period imitated more than the general shape or outline of the Stewart palaces. They also reflected a new tendency, away from the vertical living of the tower house to the horizontal, segregated accommodation of the modern house.

At Edzell, the plan was palace-like in its courtyard form and complexity with its separate ranges of residential, hall and ancillary accommodation. This rejection of communal living would continue throughout the following four centuries, eventually spreading to all other social classes. For the moment, it was the nobility alone who had the wealth and taste to follow royal fashion. The twin-turreted Stirling Forework front was also reproduced, on a politely reduced scale, at Tolquhon [21] and Rowallan. Most curious of the 'little palaces' was a temporary one built in the wilds of Atholl. When James V indulged himself in an elaborate royal hunt with the pope's ambassador, the Earl of Atholl accommodated the king and his retinue in a palace built of green timber in the forest, in strict imitation of Linlithgow with its great corner towers. After three days of hunting and nights of 'banqueting and triumph', the huge structure was deliberately set ablaze as a great firework.

Sir James Hamilton of Finnart (d.1540)

At Stirling, at last we see also the architect himself beginning to emerge from the shadow of his patron. At Linlithgow and Stirling, James V entrusted overall control of his alterations to Sir James Hamilton of Finnart, a nobleman closely related to the king. Finnart had travelled widely in France and had also acquired considerable influence, being appointed in 1539 to the new post of 'maister of werk principale to our souverane lord of all his werkis'. Finnart's scheme at Linlithgow was relatively modest, and chiefly involved the addition of a new and more convenient south entrance approached through a squat gatehouse.

Previously, the master of the king's works had been a sort of administrator: he liaised with a master mason on the direct instructions of the king. But in Sir James Hamilton of Finnart we see the hand of the architect as specialist in a form we can begin to recognise. Finnart was a very gifted Renaissance gentleman: art lover, music lover and politician. He built Craignethan [**colour plate 4**], an astonishing fortified villa, with all the latest gadgets of war: almost a rich man's toy fort. The house was set on a clifftop above the River Nethan, and comprised a castellated lodging block with a symmetrical façade and an unusual 'split-level' ground-floor hall. This was set in a fortified courtyard fronted by a wide ditch with caponier (firing house). In contrast to contemporary military fortifications, with their irregular, polygonal bastions, Finnart's symmetrical complex, with its heavy masses of masonry, seems to hark back to earlier patterns.

Although Finnart was a close friend of the king, that did not prevent him from being executed as a traitor in 1540. On his death, he had £15,000 in gold coins and this has been put forward as the reason behind the 'trumped-up' charge against him: to lay royal hands on his considerable wealth. Finnart's power and wealth had perhaps grown too soon and too great for his own good. Nevertheless, in Finnart, we see the royal grip on architectural patronage at last beginning to loosen and, with that, the unstoppable growth of the private patron, ennobled and enriched by the monarchy. The nobility of Scotland was thereafter to unleash its new-found spending power in a stunning series of architectural projects.

The relative economic decline of the burghs up to the mid-sixteenth century meant that Edinburgh and the other large burghs did not share in the prosperity of the landowning classes. There was as yet no class of wealthy burgesses, although the position would change rapidly from the later sixteenth century. The grandiose layout of the wide High Street and the Canongate, stretching from Edinburgh Castle to Holyrood, and the narrow flanking burgage plots, was already established; the mason Walter Merlzioun was responsible for paving the High Street in 1532. But the tall stone-fronted tenement houses that we now take for granted were as yet un-built. In fact, following an act of 1508, most Edinburgh High Street houses, although structurally of stone, were faced with wooden galleries and front annexes, and were only two or three storeys high; their vertical subdivision through pressure of density had not yet begun. In the Canongate, density was even lower, and there were extensive gardens.

Royal palace-building had been partly financed by feuing land to the nobility, bringing wealth thereafter to the landed classes. After the Reformation of 1560, the nobles and lairds would begin to outdo the monarchy in terms of patronage with a stunning series of feudal power statements.

'Mr Billings thinks it remarkable that the panels of their plaster ceilings should contain representations of Roman Emperors, Classic heroes, and Scripture characters, and points to these as proof that the work was executed by foreign workmen. He declares that had the designs been produced by native artists they would, as true and patriotic Scotsmen, have filled their panels with the heads of Bruce and Wallace or other national heroes. But that is a theory which requires much stronger evidence to support it. The figures used are those which invariably accompanied the revival of the Classic taste and ideas, in painting and literature, as well as in architecture. In England, France, and Germany we find the same Classic and Scripture personages represented almost to the exclusion of native worthies.'

D. MacGibbon and T. Ross,
The Castellated and Domestic Architecture of Scotland (1887–92), II, 566

The hundred years from the Reformation to the Restoration of the Stuart monarchy in 1660 was a time of great architectural complexity. Until the Reformation, the monarchy continued to dominate the production of architecture, but increasingly the power of the nobility was evident – all too evident. At Huntly Castle, for example, in 1556, the French ambassador on seeing the grandeur of the work, remarked to Mary of Guise, Queen Regent, that the earl's 'wings will need to be clipped'. And as large as it was at that time, Huntly's magnificence was only a prelude to the throwing open of architecture to an ever-expanding nobility. The licence to crenellate, to castellate and to classicise was avidly taken up by the aristocracy, and the results were astonishing in their variety and complexity.

The same period that produced the suburban villa of Pinkie House, also saw the swaggering militarism of Fyvie – for the same client. We can also contrast the suave Italian Renaissance façade of Crichton's courtyard with the supreme, turreted romanticism of the later Craigievar. Even within the work of one architect, Sir James Murray, we see quite different approaches to what appear to be similar commissions: the ordered symmetry of Murray's Pitreavie is quite startlingly at odds with his richly decorated and asymmetrical contemporary work at Winton House. However, our surprise at finding such diversity is really a product of relatively recent assumptions about the development of art and architecture: the idea that a movement will develop and unfold in an ordered progression towards the present day. There were so many factors at play – dynastic, political, religious, social, economic – that the truth is we will probably never fully understand what drove the architects and their patrons of the sixteenth and seventeenth centuries in such apparently contradictory directions.

ARCHITECTURE AND THE REFORMATION

One of the most momentous of social forces affecting architecture over these hundred years was, of course, religion. The shock waves of the Reformation of 1560 were felt culturally and politically throughout the period and beyond. In architecture, the balance of patronage was completely changed, in favour of the nobility as much as the monarchy. But what were the physical consequences? We have already seen that large-scale church building had declined after the construction of St Machar's and the shift in patronage to the Stewart monarchy, but the church's loss was really the aristocracy's gain. In 'delegating' their feudal power to the nobility, the Stewarts had created a new class of patron, with huge appetites for comfort and status. With the aristocracy split by religious differences,

Renaissance values were now promoted by a new breed of cautious administrators and middle men, able to present an acceptable faith to the prevailing régime. One of the greatest of these men was a person we will meet in many guises, Alexander Seton. Although initially trained as a priest, we first encounter him in his role of patron of the Protestant church.

In 1560, Scotland's ancient system of patronage was reformed as a parish-based system. From now on, there were no architectural requirements other than a 'preaching box', focused on the minister. In spite of attempts to bring the Scottish Church into line with English practice, the consequences for new architecture were minimal. However, the consequences for existing churches were considerable, as the reformers set about reorganising them internally for the new service, with the pulpit and the communion table at the centre. Many churches, split into separate areas and chapels, had never been designed to accommodate congregations. Churches were also 'cleansed' of ornament and much was lost in the process, although a greater loss seems to have been sustained during a second, far more severe phase of iconoclasm carried out by sixteenth-century Covenanters.

The simplest way of accommodating the new Protestant order was by the addition of a wing, making the church T-shaped. This wing was often of two storeys, with a burial aisle and/or a patron's loft. The parish church thereby entered into its new, eventually contentious, role of ancillary power-centre of the local laird. The most interesting laird's 'aisle' (range or wing) of this period was the Dunfermline Aisle, added around 1610 by Alexander Seton, 1st Earl of Dunfermline, to St Bridget's Church, Dalgety Bay [10]. At first glance the building hardly looks like a church at all. It is very much the 'office' of Seton as powerful local landlord, architecturally representing its patron as a man of scholarship and classical learning with its monumental exterior and expensive, stone-panelled interior.

Churches varied enormously throughout the later sixteenth and seventeenth centuries. However, the simple pitched-roof rectangular type – which is such a familiar Scottish landmark – received a special endorsement in 1594, when James VI built a new, free-standing chapel at Stirling for the royal christening. Unlike most parish churches, which were normally entered from one end, the Chapel Royal had a central entrance with a twin-columned portico of triumphal-arch proportions. The entire elevation was made up of paired windows in large openings, giving the composition a close resemblance to contemporary Florentine buildings with their large area of wall punctured by round-arched openings. Inside, the chapel was decorated with wall paintings, and hung with tapestries, pictures, and sculptures. There were other examples of centralised planning by individuals and by the growing burghs [11]. At Burntisland, the new dynamic relationship between the burgh and 'its' church resulted in a remarkable piece of square-planned 'rationalism': St Columba's Church (1589–96) was arranged around a central space and originally crowned

[10] St Bridget's Church, Dalgety Bay (c.1610)

[11] Skelmorlie Aisle, Largs (1639)

As the wealth and self-perceived status of the lairds grew, they began to build monuments during their own lifetimes, but commemorating their deaths. At their most grandiose, these monuments were attached as entire wings to existing parish churches as reminders of the laird's privileged position. The other main type of monument was put up in burgh churches or where no single laird prevailed. From the 1620s, these were designed as upright portals to be placed against an external wall. Greyfriars Churchyard in Edinburgh has a superb collection of this type. The most spectacular of all the monuments of the period was the Skelmorlie Aisle, Largs, built by Sir Robert Montgomery for himself: a laird's aisle incorporating a freestanding structure in the shape of a triumphal arch, containing tomb below and family loft behind and above.

[12] Geometria, Edzell Castle (1604)

With the growth of the towns in this period, we also see a complementary interest in the escape from the town – the garden. The formal Renaissance garden, with its statues, fountains and shaded walks, started to appear attached to the greater houses or villas from the beginning of the seventeenth century. Being of such a transitory nature, very little survives today from this period. The celebrated formal garden of Drummond Castle in Perthshire, for example, is a complete reconstruction of 1839 following the revival of interest in this stately age of landscape design. At Seton Palace, a 'turreted' walled garden was recorded in 1603. The most notable surviving Renaissance geometrical garden is that added to Edzell Castle in 1604 by Sir David Lindsay, Lord Edzell. Lindsay was a cosmopolitan lawyer and great 'improver' who carried on large-scale tree planting and mining on his estate. His garden was surrounded by walls originally decorated with pilasters, pediments, Stuart unionist royal symbols and carved panels depicting the planetary deities, the Virtues and the Arts. It is important to bear in mind also that gardens were perceived as 'philosophers' groves' and theatres of science.

by a pyramidal roof and a wooden steeple. At the other extreme from burgh or patron-inspired Protestant rationalism was a growing, royally sponsored anti-Presbyterianism. In 1617, James ordered the Chapel Royal, which was now located in the recognised capital at Holyrood, to be reorganised according to the Episcopalian liturgy.

HOUSING THE NEW NOBILITY

From the later sixteenth century, the small scale 'politeness' of Rowallan, Edzell or Tolquhon was largely forgotten as the major power-brokers and landowners rushed into vast architectural projects. As a direct result of the aristocracy's new status, we see a dramatic rise in the country house as a building type, along with the 'demilitarising' of the landed classes who were its patrons. In post-Reformation Scotland, the Renaissance attribute of militarism was played down in favour of the liberal arts, as Scotland moved into a phase of peace with its old enemy, England. Now, lawyers and administrators were needed, not generals. This hundred-year period also saw the end of the virtual state monopoly on architecture. The new buildings and reconstructed set-pieces continued throughout the period to take their cue from the court but, especially after 1603 and the Scottish king's departure for London, the aristocracy took on an unusually powerful role through a circle dominated by a few 'great' families: Maitland, Argyll, Seton [20], in a series not of new houses, but of lavish reworkings of earlier Baronial architecture [13 & 14].

Who designed these new buildings? After the Reformation,

James VI (1566–1625)

The reign of James VI saw a growth of links with Northern Europe, especially after James's marriage to Anne of Denmark in 1589. Gradually, links with France and Italy fell away, and were forgotten entirely by the nineteenth century, in the anti-French hysteria of the Napoleonic Wars. In Scotland, James VI extended the peerage to the greater lairds in order to increase court favour and so buttress his régime. The scene was set for the emergence of the 'improving' landlords, who were not content simply to take the rents due to them through ownership but were beginning to take a hard-headed view of their property and its potential to increase their wealth. This was achieved through the intensification or 'industrialising' of agriculture and through the capitalist establishment of coal mining, salt or lime manufacture. Crucially, too, the world began to be seen as a colony and a market place. The 'national interest' could now be bound up with the commercial in a very direct way and the issue of reconciliation with England would be increasingly affected by the 'improving' mentality. The wider enfranchisement of the nobility and their subsequent entry into the world of politics brought with it a cultural enfranchisement. The Renaissance as an idea lost its perceived power to bind the nation under an imperial monarch and instead became an influence for 'humanising' the national myth, broadening it now to include the 'people'. The sovereignty of the king – his 'divine right' to rule – had been challenged in the History of Scotland (1582) by the philosopher George Buchanan and the way was clear for an expansion of high culture – including architecture – well beyond the walls of Linlithgow and Stirling.

James VI took Renaissance classicism a step further, setting himself up as the leader of a 'Castalian Band' (Castalia, a fountain on Parnassus sacred to Apollo and the muses) of court poets. He began to write texts on the contemporary philosophical debate surrounding the divine right of kings. It was through architecture that the scope of the monarch's learning could be visually displayed. When he assumed the throne of England in 1604, James VI entered London through temporary triumphal arches in the manner of a Roman emperor. Thereafter, he sponsored a new and highly sophisticated classicism, expressed through buildings and in masques (courtly performances with elaborate architectural scenery) commissioned by his wife, Anne, and designed by Inigo Jones. But reconciliation between Scotland and England was a double-edged sword in that it initially seemed to require the reintroduction of ceremony within the church. Religion had been the driving force of Stewart/Stuart nationalism (the French spelling of Stuart was adopted by Mary Queen of Scots), but the old religion was Catholicism and that, of course, presented problems for the pro-England party. From now on, Protestantism was largely expressed through classicism, a tendency that would continue right up to the twentieth century.

[13] **William Schaw (?) with Alexander Seton: Seton Tower, Fyvie Castle, Aberdeenshire (1596–9)**

[14] **Pinkie House, Musselburgh (1613)**

Chancellor Seton's Fyvie Castle is the earliest 'revived' castellated house, but we will see that there was another side to Seton, as there was also to the Scottish 17th-century character. The staircase-hall at Fyvie was full of heraldic display, Lord Seton having 'quite a passion for that science', but at his Edinburgh villa, Pinkie House, European cosmopolitanism and liberalism flourished. The house and garden were conceived together as a place of peace: in Seton's own words, 'no place of warfare, designed to repel enemies'. At Pinkie, and at nearby Winton House (1620–7), we meet for the first time the court architect, Sir James Murray of Kilbaberton. With his learning and his new attitude to architectural types, Murray represents the gradual but continuing emergence of the professional architect from out of the shadows of the royal court. Between 1560 and 1660 the 'high' architecture was becoming the 'property' of the nobility as opposed to the crown, but they had no sooner taken control than it was to pass to burgesses, and eventually Town Councils.

[15] Linlithgow Palace, north quarter (1618–20)

Sir James Murray's flatted 'guest house' introduced a completely new building type. Between 1618 and the 1620s, Murray replaced the former north quarter with a range of self-contained lodgings.

there began a dramatic change in the range and type of buildings put up under the supervision of a designer. Eventually a 'typology' would emerge so that a bank or a court house, for example, might develop a recognisable form. For the moment, however, the possibilities for architectural form were very limited and this remained the case throughout the seventeenth and most of the eighteenth centuries. With the extension of the architectural suffrage to the nobility, the greater lairds and eventually the 'professional' architect, the main building type erected in the period was the dwelling of the aristocrat. The will to build was driven forward by a desire for comfort and, as with the Stewart monarchy, by a mixed image of old and new. The monarch took the lead in the introduction of the modern notion of privacy in a form we can recognise, with segregated bedrooms, dining-rooms, and hallways. This desire for comfort and privacy led to a movement towards more specialised planning, including self-contained blocks of lodgings, as at Linlithgow north quarter [15] and Dunottar, which allowed guests to be accommodated away from communal areas. This quest for comfort was now taken up by the aristocracy, as was the architecture of power: towers and battlements. The aristocracy also followed the monarchy in adding to existing buildings rather than building anew.

As the architectural activity of the aristocracy grew, so that of the monarchy shrank, in scale if not in prestige. The major works were those carried out by James VI at Dunfermline (in the 1590s, for his new queen), the Stirling Chapel Royal (1594), the Edinburgh Castle palace block (1615–17), and the Linlithgow north quarter (1618–1620s). The masters of works in this period now began to break out of the royal monopoly on their talents. William Schaw (Master of Works 1583–1602), James Murray of Kilbaberton (1607–34) and Sir Anthony Alexander all worked for the monarchy but, to a greater or lesser extent, worked also for themselves. Thus we see the continuing rise of the independent architect, although none of these men would come close to our understanding of an architect today. Architecture during this period entered a transitional phase which was to last well into the late-eighteenth-century world of Robert Adam. There was no simple divide of patron and designer.

[16] Huntly Castle, Huntly (completed 1610)

In both royal and landed building, the most popular way of signifying classicism was through the application of classical detail, including columns, pilasters, pediments and balustrades, no matter how 'Scottish' the building type. There was no inherent contradiction in a Scottish stair tower topped by a Renaissance balustrade as, for example, at Castle Fraser. The spread of printed French or Italian pattern books, by authors such as Serlio (available in one volume from 1566) or du Cerceau (1576–9), for the first time gave patrons and designers throughout Europe access to an international standard of detailing. Now it became necessary to 'articulate' sheer walls with details, often culled from pattern books. Within the Renaissance in Northern Europe, different countries developed their own variants of 'classical' ornament which was applied to buildings of quite different character. There was at first no attempt to compose whole buildings according to principles of proportion, framed by the orders. In the north-east of Scotland, the spectacular castles built by the Bel family of masons, such as the early seventeenth-century phase of Huntly, concentrated their pediments, turrets and other decorative features above a heavy, stepped corbel course, giving the characteristic burst of architectural flourish above the wall head.

Internally, the walls of these houses were hung with tapestries or painted. Furnishings were few and judged generally of less importance than the 'heritage' of immovable architecture and fittings. Gradually, however, a change took place in line with the

requirement for greater comfort: walls were plastered and articulated with decoration or hung with paintings, carpets were introduced, along with glazed windows, leading eventually to sash-and-case windows, the height of modernity. The changes were, as usual, seen first in the royal work. In the first part of our period, Queen Mary's apartment in Holyrood (1558–9) was ornamented with decorations all'antica (in the Antique style). The style was later followed in the most prestigious houses of the aristocracy. However this busy, essentially applied style was reformed in the first half of the 17th century with the introduction of a cooler, more architectural form of an interior decoration of ribbed ceiling plasterwork, arranged in geometrical patterns, sometimes with heavy suspended bosses; the first examples of such ceilings, dated 1617, were at Edinburgh Castle's palace block and Kellie Castle. Decoration of these ceilings included heraldic or Antique features, such as British royal symbols (for example at the Binns, c. 1630).

[17] Heriot's Hospital, Edinburgh (from 1628)

Even outwith royal building circles, a hierarchical system of patronage seems to have applied. In the case of George Heriot's Hospital, a highly complex patron–designer–contractor relationship developed, possibly because of the nature of the scheme. William Wallace and his successor as royal master mason, William Aytoun, seem to have acted as contractors, and the former may have been involved in preparation of a model and layout plan, which may have been that eventually adopted. Some stylistic features also suggest involvement by Sir James Murray in the architectural design. A whole hierarchy of design input was therefore involved in the carrying out of this one project. However, in the case of country houses and other less important projects, masons had a much more direct design role, as in the case of some of the Aberdeenshire castles built by the Bel family. In other instances, such as the houses of Alexander Seton, the patron must surely have exerted a much more forceful architectural role.

In Edinburgh in the 1620s the jeweller George Heriot – Queen Anne's jeweller – left the enormous sum of £23,000 to build a school. Following Heriot's death in 1624, his nephew, Sir Walter Balcanquhall, provided a plan for a quadrangular block, seemingly based on an example in Serlio's seventh book, with Linlithgow-like corner towers. The execution of the project was largely overseen by Wallace and Aytoun (from 1631), but what is not clear is who had responsibility for the architectural design. Much of the detail was continental in

form but other features, such as the buckle quoins, were more overtly 'Scottish'. These features, and the elevational treatment, resembling Linlithgow's north quarter with its polygonal turrets, point to Murray's involvement. With Heriot's the epoch of the non-royal urban palace had arrived: the hospitals, the prisons, the universities – even the houses of the citizens – would in the future be framed within this palace format.

[18] Edinburgh Castle (from 1566)

Increasingly, as was noticed at the Palace block at Stirling, the royal works addressed the town, stressing the role of the monarchy at the heart of the

growing city. At Edinburgh in 1615–17, the Palace block was rebuilt so as to present an outward face of ashlar symmetry high above the castle walls (seen here, top left). Inside, it was intended that there should be flatted king's and queen's apartments like Holyrood. At Linlithgow, the external

elevation, like the main external walls, was treated in a restrained manner, emphasising Linlithgow's 'closed', Renaissance courtyard aspect [15]. This suave 'castellated classical' style had a precedent in the contemporary royal palaces of Queen Anne's native Denmark.

On top of this already fluid situation was a hierarchy of project, from royal work to utilitarian building, which would determine the precise role of patron, architect and mason/contractor in each case. The designing and building of James VI's Chapel Royal at Stirling, for example, would require an elaborate chain of command with the master mason in the role of contractor only. However, this strict hierarchy was breaking down, not in favour of the mason, who was being increasingly defined as a tradesman, but in favour of the architect. The architect was set on a course of 'professionalism' that would lead to the redefinition of the master mason as sub-contractor. Sir William Schaw, a relatively wealthy laird, was appointed Master of Works in 1583. Sir James Murray, unlike Schaw, was not a laird but an artisan in origin, the son of a master wright in the royal works. He superintended and, in all likelihood, designed the new works at Edinburgh Castle [18] and Linlithgow (working with William Wallace, royal master mason 1617–31), as well as other projects such as the new Parliament House, Berwick House and his own house, Kilbaberton.

[19] James Norie: 'Taymouth Castle' (1733)

The 7th laird of Glenorchy, Sir Duncan Campbell, was one of the first to begin estate improvement in the Highlands around 1600, including commercial forestry as well as landscaping. Ominously, this 'improvement' included the outlawing and 'clearing' of the MacGregors (the Campbells' erstwhile praetorian guard) from the ever-expanding and now legally held lands. Sir Duncan's son, Sir Colin, devoted much time to ornamenting the family castle of Balloch (the present Taymouth). His enhancements included furniture, tapestries, and a series of over forty paintings (by George Jamesone and an unnamed German artist), depicting himself and his ancestors, the old kings of Scotland, and Charles, 'King of Great Brittane'.

[20] Alexander Seton (1555–1622)

The figure whose values summed up the uncertainties of the age, and who built two of its most important projects – the remodelling of Fyvie Castle (1596–9) and of Pinkie (1613) – was Alexander Seton. Seton's career included appointment as Chancellor of Scotland, creation as Earl of Dunfermline, and the assignment of a leading role in the abortive 1604 union negotiation with England. Seton was a member of the 'Octavians', a group of lawyers hired by the state to put the country's finances in order: an important member of the political establishment. After his death, Seton was hailed as 'a great humanist in prose and in poecie, Greek and Latine, well versed in the mathematicks and had great skill in architecture and herauldrie'. The story of Seton's two great projects is bound up with the politics and culture of his time, yet it stands apart as a brilliant but apparently contradictory episode in Scottish architectural history.

This complexity is nowhere better expressed than in Seton's house at Musselburgh near Edinburgh. Pinkie House **[14]** *seems to conform to neither classical nor romantic architectural ideas. But this would be to wish the architectural past arranged neatly into*
movements and styles. The main east range is a long and narrow extension of an existing tower house, quiet and square in profile, with a range of regular windows. However, Seton, with the possible assistance of Sir James Murray, also seems to have heightened the existing tower house and 'romanticised' its profile with turrets. To one end of the long range is a triple-decker oriel window overlooking the site of the Battle of Pinkie, an effect possibly conceived in the same spirit as Dunbar's picturesque overlooking of the remains of Berwick Castle. In both cases a theatre of war is presented historically, beginning a process that was to lead in time to the revisiting of Bannockburn and Stirling Bridge. Confrontation with England was, according to the prevailing policy of the time, to be rejected in favour of the reconciling 'king of peace'.

Martial imagery was played down at Pinkie, only a few years after Seton's massive tower at Fyvie had seemed to broadcast a message of war. On Pinkie's garden front, there was a striking series of tall, wallhead chimneys which suggested the lack of internal, axial divisions and therefore – the height of urbanity – a gallery. This famous gallery **[colour plate 7]** was painted with trompe l'oeil architecture in the manner of the Renaissance, a conversation piece on a huge scale, full of meaning and counter-meaning to be drawn from the illustrations of antique or mythological scenes. Now the patron's concept becomes clear, for in its iconography and its own inscribed justification, it emerges that Pinkie was conceived as a Renaissance villa – a 'retreat' from the city and a place of moral contemplation.

Gradually, throughout the seventeenth century, the aristocracy took the place of the monarch at the head of Scottish society and, effectively, as chief arbiters of taste. The aristocracy also began to lead Scotland on a more commercially orientated path to 'improvement' and industrial development. Paradoxically, or perhaps predictably, as the old world faded from view and commerce began to displace kinship, there was a renewed interest in dynastic architecture. This continued the process of 'packaging' the past and presenting it in a particular way. The aristocracy was poised between the presentation of a 'natural' order and their own wish to exploit, and therefore to change, that order.

TOWER HOUSES

Scotland's devotion to its own brand of castle-like architecture throughout the seventeenth century was unique in Northern Europe. But this adherence went very far beyond an unwillingness to shed traditional forms because of conservatism or through a fear of marauding neighbours. In such a complex political situation, the use of castle-like forms represented both a survival and a conscious revival of 'traditional' Stewart palace architecture. Internally, much of this prestige was expressed through a new segregation of living accommodation and especially through grandiose staircases, for example at Careston (c.1580), or Newark (1597–9).

The exterior was equally important. In 1632 Sir Robert Ker wrote to his son, the Earl of Lothian, offering advice on the remodelling of the family castle at Ancrum. He recommended estate improvement and the banning of activities such as football from the vicinity of the house. Clearly, new ideas of privacy were extending even to the environs of the house. Yet regarding the old tower at the centre of the complex, his son was advised to be more cautious. On the one hand, 'because the world may change agayn', windows should be kept small on the ground floor and a well should be maintained inside the house. On the other, he advised that 'By any meanes do not take away the battlement … for that is the grace of the house, and makes it looke lyk a castle, and henc so nobleste, as the other would make it looke lyk a peele' (simple fortified border tower).

In none of the building projects of the aristocracy in the later sixteenth century was the scale of the James IV/V works even approached. However, near the end of the sixteenth century Alexander Seton set about the aggrandisement of his newly-acquired house at Fyvie Castle in Aberdeenshire [13]. Working with a member of the Bel family of masons, Seton spectacularly extended an old house, dating probably from the thirteenth century. Seton's new frontage comprised flanking corner towers and a huge centre block consisting of linked round towers with a central arch. Inside, a spectacular new ceremonial approach was constructed, in the form of a stone staircase contained within a twenty-foot square space. The staircase is constructed on a series of arches springing from the newel (the central pier) and resting on the decorated consoles (brack-

[21] Tolquhon Castle, Tarves (rebuilt from 1584)

In many rebuilding schemes, there were constant echoes of the grand Stewart residences of the previous hundred years. Linlithgow's courtyard and James V's gatehouse were also evoked in the 'new wark' built by William Forbes at Tolquhon in 1584 in the form of four ranges round a courtyard, with gallery on two sides, entered by a twin-towered gatehouse. A similar plan was employed at the new-built House of Boyne for Sir George Ogilvie of Dunlugas (1575–80). Dudhope Castle in Dundee, built

from 1580, also had a twin-towered entrance and round towers at the angles; a more miniaturised two-tower gatehouse of 1567, set into the front of a small courtyard block built around a hall-house of c.1530–40, was built at Rowallan.

[22] Huntly Castle, Huntly (completed 1610)

The most monumental examples of the diagonal-towered pattern were in the north-east. At Castle Fraser, there were three main stages of development: first, a square tower at the core; second, the addition of diagonal wings (one square, one round) by c.1592; and third, in 1617–18, the elaboration and heightening of this group into a monumental composition by John Bel, mason, for Andrew Fraser. Bel heightened the round tower by all of four storeys, finishing it with a balustrade, and raised the remainder of the building to match. A broad symmetry was achieved by the building of turreted wings. The Castle Fraser tower was, as we will see, much referred to in the 19th-century Baronial revival. However, the greatest of the north-east castles was Huntly, a house which followed the same three-stage building process as Castle Fraser, but culminated in a later phase of massive additions – by George Gordon, 1st Marquis, c.1600–10 – creating a new palace of immense cosmopolitan refinement, recalling palatial French precedents. To some extent we can already contrast the architecture of the 'well-mannered' Argyll Lodging or the various Linlithgow progeny at Edzell or Melgund with the grandeur of Huntly. Gordon created suites of apartments on two upper floors (above the Great Hall), with inner chambers in the huge round corner tower and a line of oriels, spiky dormers, and tall friezes inscribed with his name and that of his wife, Henrietta Stewart. There was a particular emphasis on heraldic carving, including a vertical panel above the main entrance (with lavish Catholic imagery, smashed by a Covenanting army in 1640), and decorated chimneypieces inside.

ets) of the outer wall. The whole space is therefore carried on barrel vaulting in contrast to the elaborately ribbed vaulting of French examples such as Château de Chaumont.

Where castle complexes were dominated by a tower, the aim of horizontal expansion was severely restricted. One answer was to create a Linlithgow-like hall and tower composition, for example at Carnasserie, Argyll, where an earlier structure was enlarged in 1565–72 by John Carswell, Bishop of the Isles, using Stirling-based masons and the latest court-style classical decoration from the East. On a smaller scale, Ferniehurst Castle (rebuilt 1598) combined a two-storey main block and a four-storey tower, including a circular library in its east tower. However the most popular way of creating more space was by adding wings. At the late-sixteenth-century Duntarvie, a four-storey block was given five-storey square towers at either end, thereby creating a U-shaped plan, with a centrally placed straight flight of stairs to the first floor, an obvious 'modernising' feature. More common were the plan types which added one or two side wings to a main block, or extended it with two diagonally placed towers. For description and analysis of these buildings, the five-volume set produced by David MacGibbon and Thomas Ross between 1887 and 1892 is a delight and will probably never be surpassed, providing a basis for important research and re-interpretation by Aonghus MacKechnie and others.

Many more castles were built by the Bel family and others, in the north-east to the Huntly [22] pattern. These castles, which used a similar formula of corbel table and exuberantly castellated skyline, included Crathes (1553–96) and Craigievar [23, 24]. Craigievar is one of the Bels' most impressive architectural feats. It was a six-storey tower bought partly completed in 1610 by 'Danzig Willie', William Forbes, a wealthy Baltic trader, and finished (1626) with the help of John Bel. The castle, like many others, was originally enclosed by a small courtyard. Inside, Craigievar still followed long-established principles of tower-house design, stacking vertically no fewer than eighteen rooms and a great hall, but its exterior was brought right up to date with a typical rush of Renaissance detailing at the wallhead and incorporating the new device of a viewing platform.

[23] John Bel: Craigievar, Aberdeenshire (1620s)

[24] Philabeg: plan and section of Craigievar

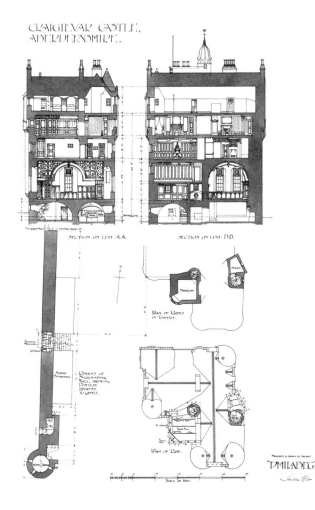

[25] Preston Tower, East Lothian
(16th c., raised in 17th c.) MacGibbon & Ross

The other main way of trying to increase accommodation in tower-based plan-types was by deepening the main tower into a plan two rooms deep, with spinal corridor, as at Drochil (from c.1578, for Regent Morton). At one of the smaller lairds' houses, Preston Tower, near Haddington, a Renaissance house was erected, bizarrely almost, on top of the existing tower.

THE FIRST CLASSICAL HOUSES

One of the difficulties with Scottish architecture is that it cannot simply be presented as a gradual progression towards a 'purer', more 'classical' style. The first experiments in classicism at, for example, Crichton Castle by the 5th Earl of Bothwell, Lord High Admiral of Scotland, were startlingly 'foreign' in their interpretation of classicism, although located within a traditional courtyard castle. The entire façade of the new quarter was carried on a loggia and articulated with faceted stone in a manner unique to Scotland, but relatively common in Italy. Typically, also, great attention was paid to the form of the staircase, which rose the full height of the building in a wide scale and platt (staircase with regular flat landings as opposed to a turnpike stair).

There was also a small group of houses or extensions built by close supporters of the official Scottish policy of uniting England and Scotland under one monarch. Two of James's most trusted supporters were richly rewarded with key English government posts and titles. These were George Home, Lord Berwick and Earl of Dunbar (from 1605); and Edward, Lord Bruce of Kinloss. Originally a lowly figure, Home was appointed Treasurer in 1601 and English Chancellor of the Exchequer in 1603. He pushed ahead James's policy of Episcopalianism and shot to fame and fortune as a result, outstripping even the old aristocracy. Both men built stately classical houses, long before William Bruce came on the scene in the 1670s. In 1607, Dunbar commissioned James Murray to design 'a sumptuous and glorious palace', Berwick House, symboli-

Sir James Murray (d. 1634)

In recent years, Sir James Murray of Kilbaberton has been 'rediscovered' as the *force majeur* of Scottish architecture from the early seventeenth century to his death in 1634. Born of lowly stock, the son of an Edinburgh tradesman in the royal service, Murray rose to a position of great influence, initially through his abilities in architecture. As we have already seen, Murray's works included the Earl of Dunbar's house at Berwick, the north quarter at Linlithgow, and the additions to the Great Hall of Edinburgh Castle. Domestic works included Baberton (originally called Kilbaberton, from 1633); Pitreavie (1630); and Winton (1620–7, for Lord Seton). As premier architect in the country, Murray was also involved in the design of the Parliament House and the reconstruction of the Abbey Kirk of Holyrood for Charles I's coronation visit in 1633. Only at Kilbaberton is Murray's direct oversight absolutely certain. Through a close inspection of the buildings we can trace Murray's characteristic approach and style. In the case of the three domestic works, the house forms a U shape around a shallow courtyard, with an entrance door situated in one or two of the angles. The crucial features of these buildings is their symmetry and their lack of traditional Baronial detailing, particularly crow-stepped gables. The applied decoration at Kilbaberton included buckle quoins, obelisks, and windows topped by sculptured pediments.

Murray's concern with classical order was largely expressed through balance and symmetry. At Pitreavie, for example, the power of symmetry is clear, for in the west wing a door to match the entrance door (including its elaborate architectural mouldings) is introduced yet it gives access only to a cellar. Baberton and Pitreavie clearly relate to one another in their tall, symmetrical form. They also relate closely to other examples of more overtly dynastic architecture, such as Innes House, which still seems to carry with it strong echoes of a fortified residence in a way that Pitreavie does not. However this overlap is yet more evident at Winton, where the wings are treated in an asymmetrical manner with crow-stepped gables. Winton seems almost a hybrid Innes/Pitreavie with its finials and ostentatious shafted chimneys but its details, such as the window surrounds and strapwork, are pure Murray. Inside Winton, the first floor has a series of three rooms with plaster ceilings featuring Stuart royal symbols; the largest of these has a massive heraldic stone fireplace, hugely overscaled.

cally overlooking the River Tweed and set within the picturesque framework of castle ruins (perhaps suggestively arranged as a reminder of now 'historic' national enmity). The long-demolished Berwick House seems to have been a flat-roofed, square-pavilioned building with large windows, not unlike the north quarter of Linlithgow or the contemporary Culross. The following year (1608), Bruce of Kinloss began his modest palace, Culross Abbey House. This was a two-storey block with tall outer single-bay pavilions and a long flat front. The whole emphasis of the building was one of calm horizontality.

THE TOWNS

As towns grew, timber as a building material was phased out, and we see the emergence of stone-fronted tenements. This takes us to the very beginning of the use of stone in 'ordinary' dwellings. In 1550, the expatriate Scot Alexander Alesius wrote that Edinburgh's Royal Mile was 'paved with level square stones' and 'lined with buildings not constructed from bricks, but natural and square stones, so that even private houses can be compared with great palaces'. The tenements themselves were generally regular and designed like the larger houses of the day. We can compare Brisbane House, Ayrshire, for example, with tenements in Edinburgh's Canongate. This was really the beginning of civic architecture, the idea of a secular public building playing its part in the ornamentation of a town. This idea had set in with the Stirling town houses: Mar's Wark of the 1570s and continuing with Argyll Lodging [29] in the early 1630s. These were 'little' royal palaces, set in the processional route to Stirling and echoing the Forework and the Palace block. The greater palaces of the expanding capital took up this idea and added to it spectacularly through the centuries.

As far as the 'ordinary' dwellings of the merchants were concerned, in most cases existing city plots were simply intensified. In Edinburgh's High Street, merchants' houses were crammed together, their tall, narrow frontages jostling for position [26]. Some of these, like the surviving Gladstone's Land, had arched, open loggias (referred to as 'piazzas' right through to nineteenth century new buildings with a similar arrangement, such as schools). Behind the street, the buildings were subdivided both vertically and horizontally. By the later sixteenth century, for example, the upper floors of John Knox House in the High Street formed a separate house reached by its own stair. However some new buildings were also designed in the form of tenement blocks. In Glasgow, the French traveller Jorevin de Rocheford commented in 1661 that 'the streets…are large and handsome, as if belonging to a new town.' The crucial development for the monumental Scottish city was the phasing out of timber and its replacement with stone and the policing of building by the Dean of Guild Courts, a kind of early planning department. Finally, stone was made compulsory for all new buildings in Glasgow and Edinburgh.

By the late seventeenth century, the four cities of today had already established a clear gap between themselves and lesser towns, with Edinburgh having a population of over 30,000. The three other cities (Glasgow, Aberdeen and Dundee) all had populations of between 10,000 and 20,000. Now at last were built the mansions of the rich who controlled the towns. They began to see their houses and public buildings as part of a civic setpiece. Once this idea had caught hold, it was the beginning of a story that would only end with Glasgow's astonishing municipal growth in the nineteenth and twentieth centuries.

For civic building, it was of course to traditional buildings that architects looked for models. At Glasgow's huge Tolbooth [30] we see the royal architecture taken over in 1625 by the burgh and set within the context of Glasgow's unstoppable ambition. But the truly great building of the period was Glasgow College [27], sponsored by the Town Council and begun in 1630. This extensive complex was arranged around two courtyards, and, like Heriot's [17], it was designed in the court-sanctioned style of the royal masters of works. At Glasgow there was also a new departure: a pattern of tenements and shallow plan row-houses developing in deference to the city and because of the need to lay down a framework for its future growth.

In the smaller burgh or barony, the 'town house' could also be used as a power statement. At Maybole Castle [28], built from the late sixteenth century as the town house of the Earls

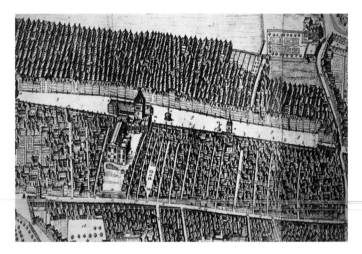

[26] **Gordon of Rothiemay: map of Edinburgh (1647)**

[27] **Glasgow College (from 1630); Slezer,** *Theatrum Scotiae*

[28] **Maybole Castle, Ayrshire (late 16th c.), R.W. Billings**

[29] Argyll Lodging, Stirling (1632 and 1674)

In the town houses of the rich there was still no clear 'type' to differentiate them from other dwellings. The largest of these houses were not dissimilar to the U-planned country houses of the period. Many have been demolished as towns have gone through wave after wave of redevelopment, but two of the best survivors are in the old town of Stirling, which was very early characterised as a set-piece of architectural heritage. These houses were Mar's Wark, town house of the Earl of Mar, 1570–2, and Argyll Lodging, built for Sir William Alexander in the early 1630s. The unfinished Mar's Wark, possibly designed by the Master of Works Sir William MacDowell, was an example of a courtier building erected near a royal palace, and closely imitating royal patterns. It also served as a backdrop for the processional route up to the Castle, for which the Earls of Mar were hereditary keepers. Mar's Wark comprises a pair of polygonal towers forming a triumphal-arch gateway, in a clear reference to the Forework, while the adjoining façade echoed the James V Palace block with attenuated shafts and sculptured panels. The nearby Argyll Lodging is certainly less of a 'public', processional statement. It was probably designed by Sir William Alexander's son, Sir Anthony (joint royal master of work), and subsequently enlarged in 1674 by the Earl of Argyll. The 1633 work comprised the extension of an 'L'-shaped block into a Kilbaberton-like 'U' layout only deeper in plan, with added turrets, and fronted by a screen wall and rusticated gateway like a French hotel. The composition was thereby regularised and given a distinctly 'civic' character in its external face of screen wall to the street. The best preserved Edinburgh town house of the period is Moray House, built for the Dowager Countess of Home c.1625, which has a gateway with pyramidal-capped piers, and gabled street façade with heavily corbelled balcony.

of Cassilis, a tall, L-planned tower is surmounted by a panelled prospect room at the top of the south wing, with three-sided ashlar oriel allowing the earl to survey 'his' burgh.

In terms of status, Edinburgh was, of course, to trump Glasgow spectacularly with the Town Council's building of the Parliament House in 1632–9 in the very heart of the capital. Designed by Sir James Murray, the project came about amid local fears that the legal profession, evicted from St Giles's by King Charles, might quit Edinburgh. Like the tolbooths, the building served several functions, including the increasingly important business of the higher law courts. Externally, the 'problem' of what the building should look like was, typically, answered by a reliance on a palace pattern, the nearest exemplar being Murray's own design for the enlargement of the great hall at Edinburgh Castle. Inside, the great-hall theme was carried through to the parliament chamber with its vast hammerbeam roof.

Politically, this part of the story ends with a revolution against Charles I's rule in 1638, which resulted in the signing of the National Covenant and the abolition of episcopacy by the Glasgow General Assembly. The events that followed culminated in the Cromwellian military occupation of Scotland in 1651–60. The consequences of those two decades for our country's architecture were dire in the extreme. Militant Presbyterians continued the unfinished business of the Reformation, even including churches built after 1560 to Episcopalian principles of design. James VI's stunning Holyrood chapel interior was ripped out. The north-east, which had been a stronghold of Episcopalianism and Catholicism after 1560, was now included as well: Bishop Elphinstone's tomb was smashed and St Machar's interior was stripped.

Only after the ending of military occupation and the re-establishment of effective monarchy in 1660 – broadcast architecturally through the 'completion' of Holyrood – would large-scale civil building begin again. This was an era in which continuity would be stressed through architecture, but the main dynamic of change – classicism – would quite spectacularly win through. Classicism would come to be understood as a complete *system*, rather than a collection of details.

[30] Glasgow Tolbooth (1625–7)
The tolbooth was the centre of a local government that had a wide remit for law and regulation enforcement. As a result, tolbooths were clearly and unambiguously 'civic' at a time when no particularly suitable pattern had yet emerged for their design. Most of the earlier examples were simple enough, comprising two storeys, a forestair and a steeple, as at Kilmaurs and many other of the smaller burghs. However, the tolbooth gave the opportunity, along with the parish church, for the burgh to advertise its scale and ambition to the world. The largest of these in the earlier seventeenth century was, far and away, that of Glasgow. Composed like a section of the Linlithgow north quarter, but with the stair-tower at one end, it was topped by a crown spire, that most triumphalist of architectural icons, probably symbolising Glasgow's royal burgh status. The main, five-storey building of the Glasgow Tolbooth was altered, then demolished in the early 20th century, leaving the seven-storey stairtower framed by 20th-century City Improvement Trust buildings.

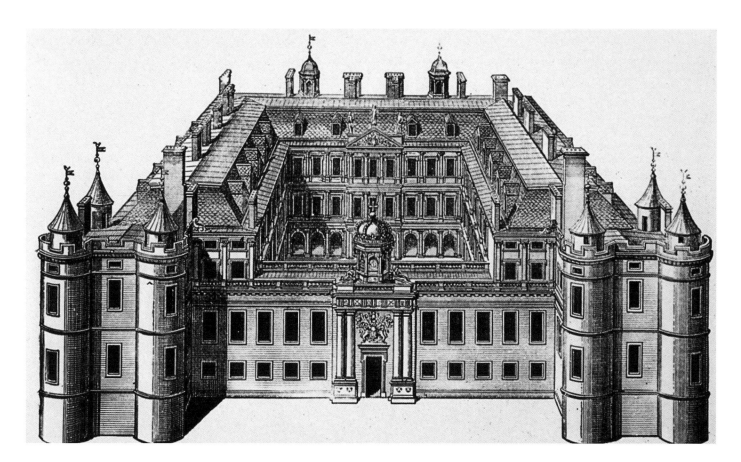

[31] **Holyrood Palace, Edinburgh (from 1670); from *Vitruvius Scoticus***

The Palace of Holyroodhouse (as it was now referred to) was Scotland's key project of the later 17th century. James V's tower of 130 years earlier was replicated, and an up-to-the-minute Palace block was put up behind an elegant classical screen. Again, the Stuart monarchy, proud of their ancient lineage, paraded the past, but also looked to the future, presenting a powerful architectural image of history and strength as well as great sophistication. The crucial decision was to retain the James V tower, incorporating it in a new, symmetrical composition. This was to set the royal seal on reform rather than revolution in country house architecture for the next thirty years.

The Rise and Fall and Rise of Romanticism

This was a century and a half of gradual but fundamental change in society and in architecture. Over these 140 years, Scotland would undergo the cataclysm of wars to emerge as a dynamic, colonising partner of England, fully committed to British imperialism. Our period begins with the restoration of the monarchy in 1660, which, after the years of military occupation, was immediately followed by a desire to 'improve'. Twenty-nine years later, with the 'Glorious Revolution' which ousted the Stuarts, Scotland's fortunes remained at first wedded to that cause, but this ancient loyalty gradually lost its force after the defeat of the 1715 Rising and the annihilation of the Jacobite claim at Culloden in 1746. From then on, Scotland's 'improvers', who strongly supported ever greater ties with England, went from strength to strength. In this period, classicism as a system of ideas ranging from politics to architecture became thoroughly ingrained in the Scottish education system. Classical morality became the very frame of reference for polite society, which throughout the eighteenth century was widening to include lawyers, professors, and even merchants. In these circumstances, classicism in architecture – the systematic use of the orders to frame buildings – was completely accepted as early as 1700.

At first, the architecture of the restored monarchy was also one of restoration, using turrets and towers to suggest the past. Even this was done, however, in an ordered, 'classical' way. Behind this mask of 'oldness' was the face of modernisation. Throughout Europe, this was an era of absolutist monarchy, but for Scotland there was a twist. The monarch was largely absent and the way was clear for an authoritarian system of government run by a kind of 'viceroy', John Maitland (2nd Earl and later Duke of Lauderdale between 1667 and 1680). Lauderdale's patronage system was then taken over by James, Duke of Albany and York (King James VII after 1685), who later established himself in Edinburgh as a princeling.

Architecture as a liberal art was becoming an essential part of a nobleman's education. From now on, the five orders would be used as a means of 'framing' all prestige buildings. In practice, this gave the palace as a building type a long-lasting authority, transposed as a form to public buildings, and even to terraces and tenements in later centuries. In the middle of the eighteenth century, growing wealth meant wider patronage, particularly in the towns. Later, there was also a huge shift in the very concept of architecture itself, from a strict understanding of the orders, to a notion of a building as the 'product' of a particular culture, whether a castle or a pagoda. On the one hand, the architect became a 'specialist', designing hospitals, prisons, even whole towns, but he also became versed in a range of different styles, each able to produce a particular effect. The idea inherent in the Scottish Enlightenment sense of having created the past as a 'place', also marked out Scotland as the country which would develop the concept of romantic nationalism under the widespread influence of James MacPherson's *Ossian* poems.

The economic growth of the later eighteenth century had huge consequences for architecture in the country, but even greater for the towns. The attitude of the landowning classes changed after the 1745 Rising and the subsequent abolition of their judicial powers. But as the landowners' power to punish was taken away, their economic power increased, and the building of planned settlements accelerated dramatically. Country houses and villas were built by the *nouveaux riches*: lawyers, merchants, and soldiers enriched by their colonial adventures. But the real growth area was the towns. In Edinburgh, Glasgow and Aberdeen, new institutions were built: assembly rooms, chambers, hospitals. In all this, the crucial development was a notion that each building within a city could relate – on equal terms – to every other. The idea of the palace, or the houses of the rich, dominating the city disappeared. In its place, a crucial new conception of the entire city as a monument was created.

[32] Thirlestane Castle, Lauder (c.1590, rebuilt late 17th c., altered mid-19th c.) (MacGibbon & Ross)
The formula used at Holyroodhouse was avidly taken up by the nobility. There were two main ways of creating the Holyrood 'effect'. An old castle could be brought up to date by realigning it, giving the building a balanced appearance, as at Glamis. More expensively, a new wing could be built, as proposed, but not executed at Traquair (c.1695). Clearly, the notion of a tower was planted deep in the Scottish architectural psyche, but it was taken to its limits at one of Scotland's most extraordinary castle-houses, Thirlestane, built c.1590 by John Maitland (Chancellor 1585–95) and partly rebuilt in the late 17th and mid-19th centuries.

Bruce's Thirlestane was concerned with dynastic display: mixing symmetry, horizontal apartment planning and castellated romanticism. The house was long and narrow, with four large rounded towers, one at each corner. Along with each of these towers was an attached stair tower in the angle, almost like four L-plan tower houses dramatically thrown together to form a rectangle. As if that were not towers enough, a further series of smaller towers was added to each of the long sides, forming an incredible rippling wall, which included four dummy towers. These imitation towers were to preserve the all-important symmetry of the composition but also to carry the astonishing new wall walk, as wide as an Edinburgh pavement.

SIR WILLIAM BRUCE

For the moment, our story is dominated not by the town house but by the country house. We take these grandiose buildings for granted, but it was only in the late seventeenth century that their form and layout was really determined. What were these houses to look like? Should the old tower houses and castellated mansions be abandoned? At first, the nobility took the lead from their absent monarch, Charles II. As part of a bid to relaunch the Stuarts, the king commissioned the gentleman architect Sir William Bruce (c.1630–1710) to 'complete' Holyrood [35]. Now Bruce was a politician, whose destiny was bound up with the monarch, who appointed him Surveyor-General of the Public Works in Scotland, France and Ireland (the English claim to the crown of France was not dropped until the eighteenth century), a version of the post held by Sir James Murray in the earlier part of the century. Bruce established himself as a landowner in 1665 at Balcaskie and in 1675 at Kinross; he was made a baronet in 1668. In 1671, he was commissioned to oversee the rebuilding of Holyrood Palace and from that point, he became the most respected architectural consultant of the day, designing his own houses, and designing or advising on many others. As a 'gentleman' Bruce would seldom, if ever, actually execute working drawings. He relied on his draughtsman, Alexander Edward, and his relationship with the masons was similar to that of Murray earlier in the century. Such a political figure as Bruce was clearly reliant on patronage. In the 1680s he was rejected by his main client, Lauderdale, and lost out completely after the dethronement of the Stuarts in 1689.

In many ways, Sir William Bruce was like another Murray, 'restored' along with the Stuarts but also rejected along with absolutist monarchy. In the future, the monarchy was to be constrained by a bureaucracy directed by politicians. For the world of architecture this meant the appearance of the yet more 'professional' architect, in the shape of James Smith. Smith was the son of a master mason who studied for the priesthood at the Scots College in Rome in 1671–5 but became an architect. In 1683 he was appointed to the royal surveyorship, and later acquired an estate at Whitehill, near Musselburgh, building a small house there. He went on to design some of the most important houses of the age, succeeding

Bruce as the most favoured architect of the establishment.

Smith's answer to Bruce's Thirlestane was another grandiose 'political' house: Drumlanrig Castle, designed in 1678–9 for the 1st Duke of Queensberry. Through massive additions, Drumlanrig took on a great quadrangular form, reminiscent of Holyrood with its bold outer towers and calmer central section. We can see that, by this time, the issue of scale or 'politeness' in relation to the royal works was almost entirely irrelevant. Instead, by building lavishly, it was possible to underscore, or to create, a royal connection.

After Drumlanrig, we see Scottish architecture take one of its characteristically sudden changes of direction. Smith also designed in the 1680s–1700s two of the greatest classical projects of the age: the remodelling of Hamilton Palace, from 1684 to c.1700, for the 3rd Duke and Duchess of Hamilton, and that of Dalkeith Palace, 1702–5, for Anne, Duchess of Buccleuch and Monmouth. At Hamilton, the decision was taken to retain some of the old house at the north, but to 'mask' it with a new U-shaped courtyard, whose long wings had the air of a great French hôtel. As at Thirlestane, a surviving duchess carried on with the huge scheme, including the interiors which were completed in 1701.

Clearly, for the Hamiltons – Scotland's premier family – continuity and dynasty were taken as read. Their palace at Hamilton was on a monarchical scale of splendour, by far the largest private project of the age. The sheer scale of the massive portico was beyond anything ever attempted: being freestanding, it was all show and expense, unlike the superimposed orders even of Holyroodhouse. At Dalkeith Palace, the Duchess of Buccleuch tried to compete, but on a smaller budget. She instructed Smith to deliver a palatial Dalkeith, with appropriately grand state apartments. However, the money would not stretch to Hamilton's serene grandeur. The house as built had an unwanted compactness and verticality, as well as an obviously cheaper surface treatment of render to the wings. The huge portico dominated the much smaller façade of Dalkeith and only seemed to heighten the contrast with Hamilton. Inside, the most important room, the double-height Great Dining-Room, had to be put on a different floor from the rest of the state rooms.

[33] The 3rd Earl of Kinghorne

Nothing could have prepared the unsuspecting visitor for Glamis Castle, a building designed by the last of the old-style patrons. Glamis was an L-planned tower house, regularised and brought spectacularly up-to-date in the late 17th century by the addition of a wing and the placing of the entrance at the meeting of the two wings. It was transformed into a great, V-planned Baroque palace, in line with current European trends in architecture. Yet it was built around the same time as the strict classical simplicity of Smith and McGill's Strathleven House in Dumbartonshire. So why build a 'castle' at this late stage? This is to beg an interesting question about the dynamic of fashion. We know that the owner/designer of Glamis, the Earl of Kinghorne, did not 'delight to live in his house as in a prisone', but that, ignoring 'Public Architecteurs', his 'great desyre' was 'to continue the memorie of my familie'.

[34] Glamis Castle (19th c. photograph)

Showing part of the interior of Glamis, stripped back in the late 19th century, re-creating an imagined past.

Alongside his enlargements of Hamilton and Dalkeith, Smith also designed a number of smaller houses for would-be lairds, such as himself. Most of Smith's villa-sized houses were cut-down versions of large country-seats, including his own house at Whitehill (1689, renamed Newhailes in 1707 and subsequently expanded). This was a two-storey house, with a tall roof, simply detailed, advanced centrepiece and pediment

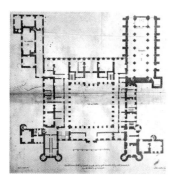

[35] Plan of Holyrood Palace, Edinburgh; from *Vitruvius Scoticus*

Strictly speaking, a proper 'state apartment' was intended only for the monarch's use, and therefore provided an ideal symbol of hierarchy. In reality, the apartment was a suite of 'best' rooms, mostly for show, in the largest houses or palaces. By 1700, a

typical Scottish great apartment might begin with a stair of the Holyrood, open-welled type, reaching a great dining-room (the largest room in 1700, but increasingly giving way to the drawing-room during the 18th century), drawing-room, and bed-chamber with dressing-room and closet. The fashion for such rooms filtered down to lesser houses never likely to be visited by royalty. The state/great apartment concept provided an ideal symbol of absolutist royalism, as well as of landed power. It was in this period of restored hierarchy that servants began to approach their new role as 'employees' in the modern sense, rather than part of the house-hold or 'family'. Fewer members of the

aristocracy were now prepared to wait on their 'betters' and with this new distinction came a need to separate the family from the servants and their duties. Increasingly, the family wished to be served but not to be seen by the servants, a concern taken to an aston-ishing extreme in the 19th-century country house. The creation of this new internal order became the business of the architect, and this again added to

his 'professional' credentials. Bruce himself excelled in this area and he experimented with adjacent servants' rooms and backstairs at Kinross **[36]** and Thirlestane, a tradition taken over from the tight service stairs of tower houses like Craigievar or Drochil.

[37] Sir William Bruce: central section of plan for Hopetoun House, near Edinburgh (1702); from *Vitruvius Scoticus*

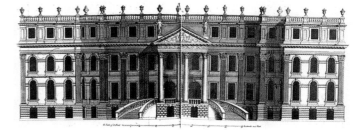

[36] Sir William Bruce: Kinross House (1679–93) Plan drawn for Sir John Bruce, son of the architect

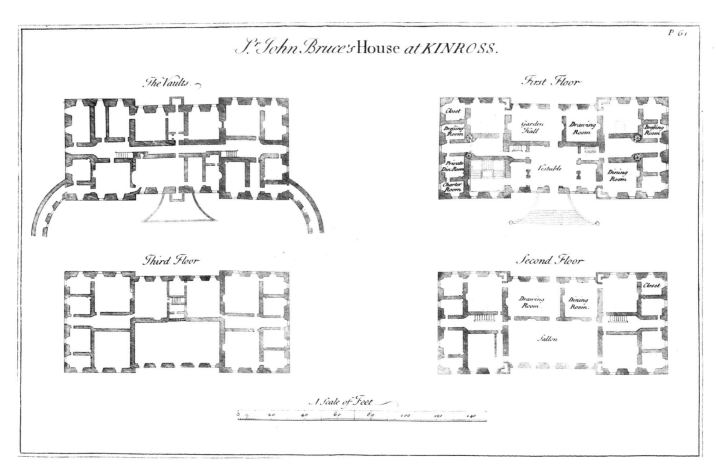

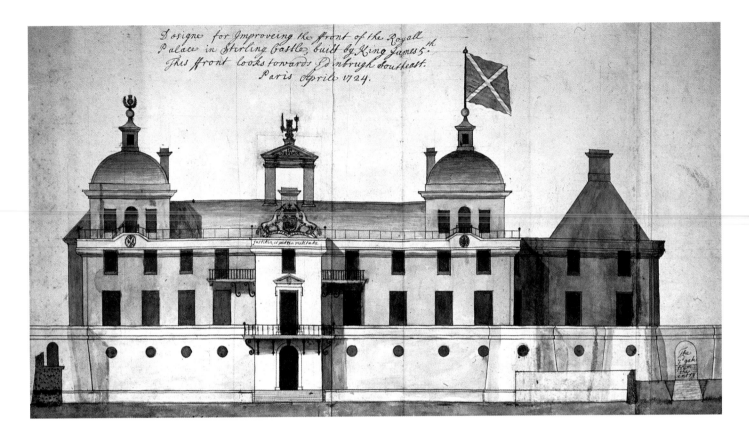

above the wallhead. What was important was that the house managed to make a 'refined' statement without being too expensive, a sure sign that 'architecture' was filtering down the social scale.

Anticipating the planning of towns, planning was now extended well beyond the confines of new buildings. The very notion of 'setting', which we take so much for granted, was played out in this period, largely under the influence of Slezer, a Dutch surveyor who helped introduce the concept of ordered layout, seen in his 'bird's eye' views of towns and country seats [3], with unwanted visual intrusions edited out. It was a small step actually to get rid of such intrusions. This notion was later taken up in the towns: buildings like St Giles' or Heriot's were 'improved' by demolishing adjacent buildings and creating aprons of urban space. In the country, gardens were also being opened up into one large space, to suggest greater grandeur. Setting was all part of a drive towards a more ordered lifestyle in which each activity had its 'place'. For the great houses, that meant for the first time creating rooms of state for the accommodation of royalty.

[38] Stirling Castle, Palace block, unexecuted scheme of 1724

Between the grandeur of Hamilton Palace and the continental sophistication of the first Hopetoun come the careers of two very different types of Scottish architect. One – the Earl of Mar – was an aristocratic would-be designer of royal palaces, the other two – James Gibbs and Colen Campbell – represented more practical tendencies connected with the new political order. The Earl of Mar was a very complex figure, known chiefly for his leading role in the Old Pretender's 1715 Rising. Ultimately, that campaign left him an exile with little to do but prepare vast architectural schemes. Although never built, these schemes were influential. Mar belonged to the courtly class of gentleman-architect who saw architecture connected to 'improvement' as well as to matters of taste, along with a reaffirmation of classical leisure as an end in itself. His projects were grandiose but bold evocations of Antiquity, and amongst a host of unexecuted schemes, the most practical is that for a proposed remodelling of the Palace block at Stirling Castle in 1724. Here, we get a strong sense of the neo-classical repose produced by balanced wings, less evident in his more Baroque composition for a 'Royal Palace' published in Vitruvius Scoticus. Not one of Mar's designs was built, but he did manage to influence at least one important Scottish house.

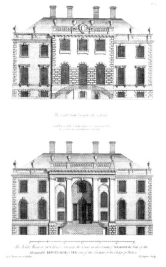

[39] House of Dun, Angus (from 1724)

At House of Dun, the exiled Mar worked in collaboration with Alexander McGill and William Adam to produce, initially, a tower-like, centralised plan in 1724. Construction began in 1730, substantially to Mar's design, although with a triumphal-arched centrepiece, rather obviously added. Internally, a remarkable plasterwork scheme was installed in 1742-3 by Joseph Enzer. This, it seems, comprised a complete Jacobite decorative cycle, portraying the peace that, in the opinion of Jacobites, would follow restoration of the Stuart monarchy. The whole project was executed under the direction of the top Hanoverian architectural post of Mason to the Board of Ordnance, held by William Adam.

Dalkeith, Drumlanrig, Hamilton Palace and Hopetoun House [37] were statements of the great families, but architecture was now filtering down to a smaller, sophisticated type of country house or villa. Kinross House, designed in the 1680s, pointed in this direction. At Kinross, Bruce achieved an elegantly simple but brilliant synthesis of planning, architecture and landscape. Externally, he created a compact monumental 'box', its wide 'pavilions' greater than its centre and articulated with Corinthian pilasters. Kinross also established a new type of stone monumentality which even Palladio's buildings – to which Kinross refers – had not possessed. Explicit historical references were kept away from the building, but for the first time, appeared framed in a landscape setting: the central axis of Kinross was centred on Loch Leven Castle, the prison of Mary Queen of Scots [**colour plate 8**].

From 1698, Bruce began a last major commission, Hopetoun House. In 1698 Lady Margaret Hope commissioned a new house for her son, Sir Charles Hope (later Lord Hopetoun). This was a smaller, geometrically-planned 'pavilion' rather than a 'seat', and in 1702-3 Bruce was brought back to recast it in a much more imposing manner. Grandiose colonnades were to join the main building to service blocks. However, this was a family on the up-and-up. By the 1720s, before the Bruce scheme was complete, Lord Hopetoun would already have begun completely refacing it to a yet grander design of his own [37].

After Hamilton Palace, the country seat with its state rooms and grandiose planning would never be the same again. The most obvious differences took place in the apartment, which had by now lost its political relevance. At Hopetoun House (from 1721) the state rooms were huge, but now they took on a new function as a picture gallery, with the paired arrangement of private rooms necessitating a vast horizontal show front. Within great apartments, the grandest rooms were now the dining- and drawing-rooms, which by 1720 had become equal in size. The status of the bedchamber, to which the drawing-room (or 'withdrawing room') had originally been subservient, was now changing rapidly into the private space familiar to us today. In the smaller houses, however, the bedchamber was regarded as a suitable room for receiving guests until well into the eighteenth century.

[40] Mavisbank House, Midlothian (1923–6)

In the design process at Hopetoun which closely involved the client, we begin to see the flowering of the 'gentleman-architect', the man of taste. Perhaps we are also seeing the beginning of the monopoly of architecture by men in the time after the great women patrons such as the Countess of Dysart, the Duchess of Hamilton, and the Duchess of Dalkeith. Sir John Clerk of Penicuik, who built his villa on Roman lines at Mavisbank (1723–6), is the prototype 18th-century connoisseur and improver: musical composer and arbiter of taste, coal master and agriculturalist, who created for himself a pious neo-Roman lifestyle. As at Hamilton, but on a smaller scale, his wealth came from the appalling slavery of coal-mining and it is worth noting here that 'improvement' referred only to the increasing of profit for the landowner. It was not until much later that the issue of poverty was addressed. Out of Clerk's wealth came a revival of the 'true antique taste', an exquisite five-bay, two-storey villa described by Clerk's architect, William Adam, as 'a very small Box, and Genteel too'. Mavisbank developed Bruce and Smith's architectural statements in country-house design, made through refinement, rather than scale and display. It was the client at Mavisbank, rather than the architect, who drove the scheme in the direction of elegant simplicity. William Adam wanted the house to be taller, but Clerk, rejecting once and for all the romanticism associated with high turrets, said that would have made it 'look like a tower'.

[41] Edinburgh Royal Infirmary (1738–48)

In the 1730s William Adam also designed a series of increasingly ambitious public commissions: the Orphans' Hospital (1734), George Watson's Hospital (1738), and the Royal Infirmary (1738–48), shown in the process of demolition. Adam's Glasgow University Library (1732–45) was civic in character, with a pedimented front and small Corinthian portico. At Dundee Town House (1731–4) Adam employed a central steeple and regular 'hall', while the ground floor was arcaded, recalling the 17th-century town house of the Provost.

William Adam (1689–1748)

As a professional architect, William Adam [**colour plate 15**] dominated architecture in Scotland from the 1720s until his death in 1748. The foundation of Adam's success was his achievement as an industrialist and contractor. He was appointed Mason to the Board of Ordnance in 1730, and thereby landed the biggest building project of the day, Fort George [**colour plate 10**]. Adam also made his mark as a general consultant on 'improvement': in 1737, the Duke of Hamilton wrote to him: 'Of my coal: perhaps it may turn out as you seem to flatter me it will; if so cubes, temples, obelisks etc., etc. will go the better on'. Adam styled himself 'architect' from 1720 and rapidly built up a specialised library. For the first time, Adam also proposed the publication of a kind of 'directory' (rather than a textbook) of Scottish architecture, *Vitruvius Scoticus,* begun in 1727 but not published until *c.*1812.

Adam's work began at Gladney House, Linktown (1711), an old-style house that he and his family occupied until 1727. In his later rebuilding of Floors (1721–6, for the 1st Duke of Roxburgh), a more up-to-date solution was found and its horizontal format was repeated in Adam's unexecuted plan of *c.*1740 for Preston Hall. This new horizontality found its most serene expression at Hopetoun (1721–48), where the front of the Bruce composition was demolished, and replaced by a new entrance front, recalling the grandeur of Hamilton Palace, but failing to manage financially the free-standing portico.

The most confident of Adam's medium-sized houses was Arniston, begun in 1726 and partly completed in 1733, for the influential lawyer Robert Dundas; it was fully completed to a different plan in 1754–8. Arniston's main façade is in the key-blocked manner of James Gibbs. Inside, is a 'theatrical' series of Baroque spaces with exuberant plasterwork by Joseph Enzer. At the top of the house, above the hall, is the library, pilastered and lined with busts.

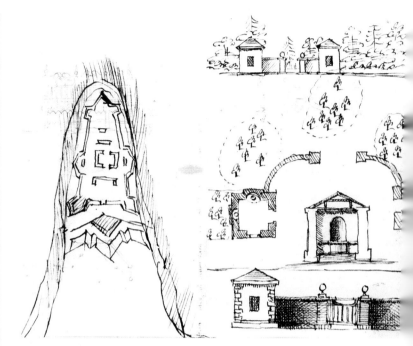

[42] Robert Adam: sketch of Fort George

In terms of sheer volume of work, William Adam's greatest projects were carried out under General Wade, the army commander-in-chief in Scotland. Adam was to profit hugely from this work, which included a share of the massive government road and bridge-building programme of 1725–37. Most of Wade's bridges were standardised affairs, but the more prestigious estate and town bridges were specially designed. The five-arched Aberfeldy Bridge over the Tay, with its obelisk-crowned cutwaters was the greatest of these. An inscription on the bridge invites the reader to 'see what the royal protection of George II is worth!'

After the 1745–6 rising, Adam was awarded his biggest military contract of all, intended as a demonstration of Hanoverian power in the Highlands: the building of a small fortified town sketched by Robert Adam (above) alongside an unrelated design for gate lodges and a screen wall. The huge complex was built over two decades (1748–69) under the supervision of the Adam family: first William, then John, Robert and James. The little 'town' was axially planned and centred on a square flanked by three-storey tenements. A chapel was built at one end of the main axis (1763–7), and the complex therefore had all the elements of a planned town like Inveraray. It is this need to order and to plan which is the main theme of Scottish architecture for the next two hundred years.

TOWN PLANNING AND PLANNED TOWNS

Until the late seventeenth century, the cities had been running in second place to the countryside in terms of building activity. However, in Edinburgh, during the late seventeenth and early eighteenth centuries, future patterns of urban development were already being worked out: the dense tenement block and the row house or 'terrace' (the term 'terrace' to describe a connected row of dwellings is derived from the Adam brothers' controversial Adelphi Terrace in London [**colour plate 11**]). Scottish urban housing layouts were distinctive in that they abandoned the long, narrow medieval plot in favour of street block development. It was in the centre of Edinburgh (and in Leith) that there first began to emerge a monumental type of purpose-built, collective dwelling-block, prompted by the capital's burgeoning economy.

The first steps in this process were taken from the 1670s in a series of tenement blocks built by Robert Mylne and James Smith. The first of these was Mylne's Land, Leith (1678), a four-storey block with attic and basement. Later, Mylne Square, in Edinburgh's High Street (1684–8), was the first to break out of the medieval layout by building across several closes in a unified design. Also important for the future was the use of ashlar facing with harled rubble at the rear, anticipating the complex hierarchy of stone facing developed over the coming centuries. The houses, intended exclusively for the rich, attempted to compress elements of a great apartment into a tight plan: accommodation varied from dining-room, three bedrooms, closet and kitchen to dining-room, outer hall, four bedrooms, closet and three cellars.

The success of Mylne's Square was repeated at nearby Mylne's Court. In the front range, key features of later Scottish middle-class tenements were charted out. This broad, shallow building, arranged along the street building line, is faced in ashlar, with plain unbroken eaves, unlike the continental tenements with their generally heaped-up profile. Inside, a wide staircase gives access to two houses on each floor. By the end of the eighteenth century much of the High Street had been transformed into a succession of ashlar tenements, some of great height – ten storeys or more – on a continuous wall plane.

In these houses, as in the tenement blocks built for the merchant classes of nineteenth-century Glasgow, there was a rapid increase in specialised room use and lavishness of furniture and other fittings. The building of individual dwellings in rows was rarely contemplated at this time. The first such developments were in Edinburgh and, planned in squares, were influenced by contemporary London; early examples included Argyle Square (completed *c.* 1742) and Brown and Adam Square (both from the 1750s).

[43] Stirling Tolbooth (1703–4)
The typical earlier eighteenth-century public building was the tolbooth: the basic pattern consisted of a meeting room above a vaulted ground floor, with steeple. This formula was retained, but a new formality was introduced in Bruce's design for Stirling Town House where the building's 'townscape' function was reinforced by the hierarchical use of ashlar on the main elevation and rubble on the side. On the front façade, a campanile-type tower similar to that of Glasgow College was linked to a three-storey classical block. The Glasgow College model of a tolbooth steeple remained highly influential as a model for civic order, even into the 18th century, but a new, more rigorous civic discipline was now being applied. Work was becoming time- as opposed to task-orientated, particularly with the later introduction of the factory system. The provision of public clocks in Glasgow became the subject of a great political debate as the municipality widened its 'police' role to include civic order.

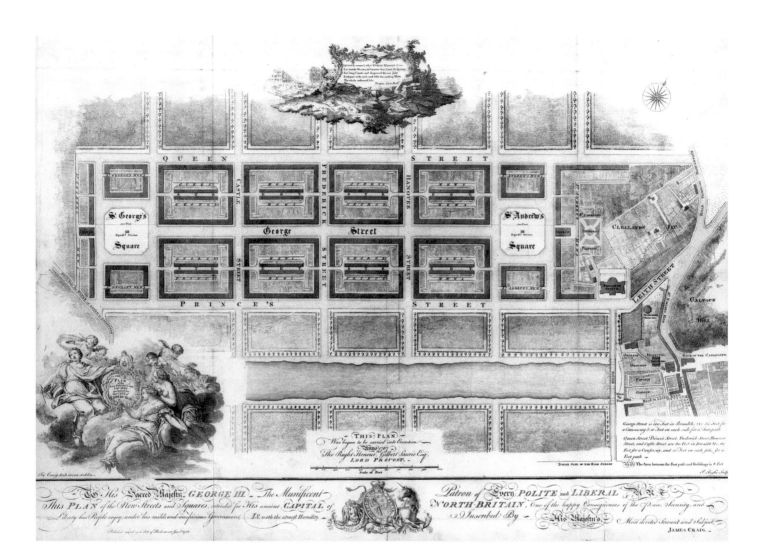

[44] James Craig: plan of
Edinburgh New Town (1767)

James Craig's competition-winning design for Edinburgh New Town was, above all, rational. It also carried a political message of improvement and progress promoted through union with England. An earlier scheme for the New Town was planned in the shape of a Union Flag. However 'rational', the new Edinburgh soon began to acquire a deeply romantic image. Its unremitting geometry was soon to be broken up in the face of a growing desire to fuse nature with planning.

[45] Robert Adam: north side of Charlotte Square, Edinburgh (from 1792, completed 1820)

EDINBURGH NEW TOWN

From the early part of the seventeenth century, towns and cities throughout Europe were under pressure to expand. Most were constricted by city walls whose defensive function was disappearing. By contrast, Scottish cities had long abandoned the defensive wall, apart from the minor defences built around Edinburgh in the aftermath of Flodden. Edinburgh's expansion was instead restricted by geography. Having achieved privacy at their country seats, the landed classes were demanding exclusive living areas in town, distanced from the disease and crime of the old centres. The problem was how to achieve separation. Land-owners and the rich were giving up their houses in town for peripheral villas in an early example of suburban flight. As in the twentieth century, the city's answer was to fight back, to 'reform' the city. Initially, as we saw, an attempt had been made to create exclusive zones *within* the existing city in purpose-built tenement blocks. In the 1750s the decision was finally taken to vault beyond the bounds of the Old Town, by creating a completely new suburb for the rich: the Edinburgh New Town. It was not, however, a new idea. This concept was directly based on late seventeenth and early eighteenth-century suggestions such as James VII's, as far back as 1688.

The aim of the New Town was to attract the rich from their villas and from the existing town, restricting the new suburb to 'people of fortune and a certain rank'. It was not intended to empty the Old Town, but to put the merchants in their 'place' in a country still wedded to landed interests and concerned about the moral basis for a commercial polity. Indeed, a centrepiece of the new plans was a Merchant Exchange, located in the heart of the Old Town. Built from 1753, and subsequently taken over by the Town Council as the City Chambers, the Exchange had a U-shaped, pedimented courtyard front of five storeys, not unlike a French or Dutch town house with its architectural screen wall.

Non-commercial public buildings were also incorporated within the overall residential layout of the New Town: churches were to terminate either end of the axis. Other public buildings were added in James Craig's [44] later versions, and by a combination of design and historical accident, Edinburgh New Town took on a startlingly original form. Unlike, for example, French new towns, there were no buildings of state in the orig-

inal plan. As a result, there was little hierarchy in positioning, although there was a failed attempt to put a church at the 'head' of the scheme (replaced, to the dismay of the Town Council, by the Dundas mansion). Lacking a fixed hierarchy to refer to, a far more 'democratic' design was possible in the Modern Athens. What was just as remarkable as the formal force of this grand plan for a new 'city as monument' was the consistency with which it was carried out over the following decades, through increasingly restrictive development controls by the Town Council and the private land-owners and trusts concerned.

In a continuing expansion of the role of the architect, the layout and the elevation of proposed schemes were incorporated at the feuing (leasing) stage. Developers now had to buy in to pre-designed schemes, such as James Craig's plan for the east end of Princes Street. In 1791 Robert Adam, at the instigation of the Town Council, took the idea of unified design to its limit in his design for the sides of Charlotte Square. Now the 'palace-front', based on the Adam brothers' less than successful London adventures, had truly arrived. Charlotte Square [45], which seemed to recall the massive ashlar monumentality of Kinross, set the tone for the next phases of New Town development.

The juxtaposition of the Old Town and the New laid the basis for an eventual revaluation of the Old Town as something valuable because of its 'oldness'. In a series of projects by Robert Adam in the 1780s and 1790s, old and new were dramatically brought together in schemes which involved vertical 'layering' of urban space. The essence of Adam's proposals was that of multi-level planning around 'bridge streets', an idea influenced perhaps by Renaissance utopian schemes such as Leonardo da Vinci's concept of ground-level commercial life and upper-level for the use of 'gentlemen'.

In engineering terms, the most ambitious of these proposals was South Bridge [46], a nineteen-arched structure over a thousand feet long, designed by Alexander Laing to link the Old Town with extensions to the south, continuing the line of North Bridge. As in Aberdeen, road communications had been carried out on the lines of a kind of inner ring road around the natural obstacles of the topography. The North Bridge / South

[46] Robert Adam: plan for South Bridge, Edinburgh (1785)

Bridge was therefore a highly modern but neo-Roman piece of engineering which levelled out Edinburgh's geography on a gigantic causeway of development. Robert Adam had immediately seen the economic and architectural potential of the scheme: his 'one connected Design', in which 'every separate House makes only a part of the whole'.

In the end, the hopes of the New Town promoters for a suburb of land-owners' houses were not realised. Although a few aristocrats did build their town houses there, merchants and professionals were by far the dominant groups. However, the New Town was by no means a commercial failure. Its proposed development was based on an old hierarchy that was being undermined and, instead, its houses became one of the key areas for the cultural expression of the new middle class.

Inside the new middle-class dwellings there was a new restraint in decoration: interiors were understated, with white painted ceilings and woodwork, plain walls, cast plaster friezes and ornaments. The interests of landscaping were served by the creation of a network of pleasure grounds, especially after 1800; the first enclosure of a garden, in St Andrew Square, took place in 1770.

TOWN PLANNING IN THE COUNTRY

The mania for improvement was paralleled – if not in fact prompted – by land-owners in the creation of rural planned settlements. Examples from the late seventeenth century included Newton Stewart (1670s) and Gifford. The most ambitious effort was a later project by the Duke of Argyll at Inveraray [colour plate 13], as part of his vast campaign of agricultural and estate improvements. The building of his new castle involved the enforced removal of nearby tenants to a new planned town. Significantly, the ducal castle did not sit in an axial relationship with the town. The first buildings were commenced by John Adam in 1751, in the form of a grand 'façade' to the north, made up of a town house and an inn flanking the arched entrance to an estate 'mall'; the eventual, cruciform plan was drawn up by Robert Mylne in 1774 and developed with rows of dwellings, including tenement blocks.

Later, a dramatic explosion of improvement-based settlement-building took place in the north-east. John Baxter laid the new town of Fochabers from 1776 on a grid plan, again with the church as its focus. Elsewhere in the north-east, the density of settlement foundation was such that two grid-plan new towns, New Keith (founded by the Earl of Seafield c.1750) and Fife Keith (by the Earl of Fife, 1817), stand right next to each other. New settlement-building also resulted from land-owners' forced movements of tenants for 'amenity' reasons, as Ker had advised at Ancrum over a century before and as Argyll put into practice spectacularly at Inveraray.

Some planned settlements were more specifically dedicated to industry. The boldest of all was New Lanark, an integrated group of six-storey cotton mills and workers' tenements, built from 1785 by David Dale (in partnership with Richard Arkwright) in the romantic setting of the Falls of Clyde. Beyond Scotland, the New Town formula of planned settlement spread its influence far and wide. For example, William

Hastie, who travelled to Russia at Charles Cameron's invitation in 1784, and assumed charge of the imperial city-planning service between 1808 and 1832, planned countless new towns across Russia on the grid-like patterns established by Craig's Edinburgh scheme.

PUBLIC BUILDINGS

We have seen that the 'country seat' dominated the architectural scene until the 1720s. Indeed it was the strength of this building type as an icon which undermined municipal attempts to bring the land-owners into Edinburgh New Town. Between 1720 and 1800 a major shift took place, both in the status of the country house and in the public building. Nevertheless, the urban architecture that was put up in the late seventeenth and early eighteenth centuries strongly hinted at the regularised and formalised future of town planning. In the 1660s–80s, the Canongate in Edinburgh had become the place for courtiers' town houses. The foremost example was the almost tenemental-scaled Queensberry House, built from 1681 as the town 'lodging' of Lauderdale's brother (the house was sold on, in 1686, to the 1st Duke of Queensberry). Later town houses were much less grandiose, with few attempting to dominate the urban scene. In Edinburgh, William Adam's town house for Lord Minto (1738–43) was compact and geometric, but had ingeniously planned and suitably grand public rooms.

From the mid-1770s, the economic revival of Scotland enabled Robert Adam to become involved with a series of grand projects in Edinburgh and Glasgow. In Edinburgh, Adam built two great public institutions – Register House and Edinburgh University – which were inspired by the model of the palace façade, rejecting the now old-fashioned idea of the U-shaped courtyard, as seen in the Merchant Exchange of only twenty years earlier. Adam's plan for Register House (1771) brought all the population records of Scotland under one roof: a rationally-planned, domed rotunda within a quadrangle. The first section was built in 1774–90; the whole building was completed in 1822–34 by Robert Reid.

In contrast to this restrained display, Adam's University College design [48] had a triumphal character, reflecting

[47] **Tron Kirk, Edinburgh (1633, altered 1785–7, steeple 1828)** *Late 17th- and early 18th-century churches were now firmly attuned to the reformed tradition of plainness and modest size, although burgh churches could express burgh aspirations, as we will see. For the most part the churches employed an austere classicism, sometimes with Gothic elements, as at Edinburgh Tron Kirk, which was later reduced in size on Robert Adam's advice in order to create an unbroken North Bridge–South Bridge axis. Larger churches might have a steeple, situated either centrally on the long axis in the Edinburgh Tron Kirk manner (as at Gifford, c.1710, possibly by Smith and McGill), or on an end gable, in the pre-Reformation manner seen recently at Anstruther Easter Church (1634–44).*

The years after 1715 saw, in many cases, a continuation of these older-established patterns. 'T'-shaped churches with a steeple on the long side included Smith and McGill's monumental New Church, Dumfries (1724–7). Experiments with centralised plans continued, most notably at William Adam's Hamilton Parish Church (1729–32), comprising a Greek cross inscribed in a circle, one arm being porticoed; and at John Douglas's octagonal Killin Church (1744). However, the growing cities now produced church designs of temple-like proportions. At St Andrew's Parish Church, Glasgow (1737–59), designed by Allan Dreghorn, the influential Glasgow architect–businessman, in collaboration with the mason Mungo Nasmyth, a giant portico was matched with a Gibbs steeple. Gibbs himself returned to Aberdeen to design a church there – St Nicholas West, in 1752–5 – which followed the same rectangular plan.

[48] Robert Adam: elevation for
Edinburgh University College (1789)

[49] Robert Adam: plan for
Bridewell prison (1791–5)

In 1791, Adam began what was probably his most remarkable design: the Bridewell prison. The Bridewell philosophy of incarceration, which emphasised reform over punishment, might have suggested a severely neo-classical expression. Indeed, the panopticon plan Adam designed (at the suggestion of the celebrated Utilitarian philosopher, Jeremy Bentham) for the Bridewell, with its comprehensive provisions of surveillance, was, above all, 'rational'. The chosen architectural style for the Bridewell was, in the event, a manner similar to Adam's 'castles', and inspired chiefly by Scottish Renaissance works. None of the surviving designs for the Bridewell relates exactly to the finished building, which stood on the site now occupied by Tait's St Andrew's House [110]. The aim of the Bridewell's romantic form was perhaps to exalt the 'untamed' quality of Calton Hill as a foil to the rational world of the New Town. The Bridewell was also doubtless related to the castellated variant of Adam's 1791 Calton 'bridge-street' proposal.

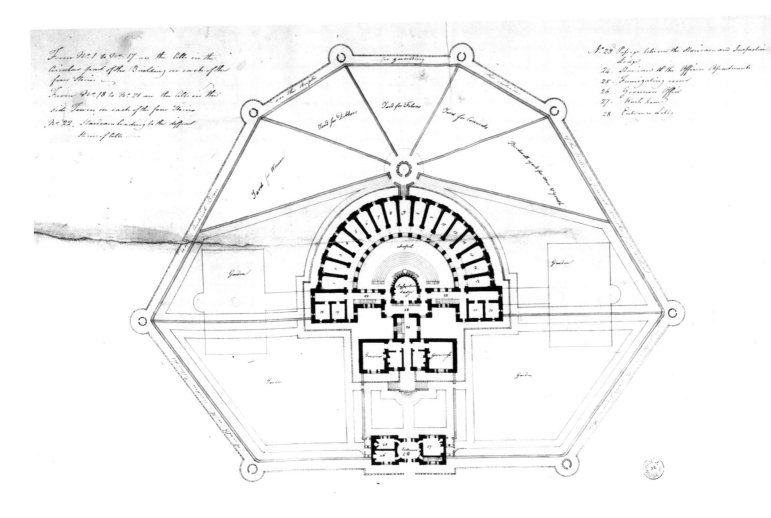

Adam's move to a more assertively romantic manner. This was not a government commission, but almost a personal crusade for Adam; he wrote in 1789 that 'I have been infinitely more activated by the motive of leaving behind me a monument of my talents, such as they are, than by any hope of gain whatever.' His plan envisaged a courtyard block, the main east façade with projecting wings and central portico featuring six columns formed of gigantic single pieces of Craigleith stone, carried to the site on specially made wagons. Building began in 1789 but halted in 1793, for several decades, through lack of money. As Sir Nathianiel Wraxall noted in 1813, 'The front as it now stands presents a very majestic appearance, but it is more like a palace for a sovereign than a college.' It had originally been proposed that the then-vacant Holyrood could be converted for the University, and there is something of that building's grandeur about Adam's executed scheme.

There were also several monumental proposals by Robert Adam for Glasgow in the last year of his life (1791–2). This series of projects would be of the greatest significance for the future, in whetting the appetite of Glaswegians for more grandiose planning of their booming town. Glasgow, with its entrepreneurial flair, avidly responded to the commercialism of Robert and James Adam's proposals: most of them included ground-floor shops, which, as today, helped finance residential and public schemes. In one scheme, for the Tron Kirk, they offered the alternative of keeping or demolishing the Tron steeple and erecting shops through which the church would be reached. The most important of the Adams' Glasgow public buildings was the Infirmary (1792–4) [134]. Here, the main elevation seems in some ways heavy and conservative, but also recalls the earlier, more vigorous hybrids such as the south front of Kedleston or the anteroom at Syon: projects all linked by their neo-classically severe grandeur. Robert and James's Glasgow proposals also included an unusual scheme of 1791 for Barony Church [right, 134], with a Fyvie-like triumphal arch with gable, caphouse and optional crowsteps (built in a different form and demolished 1889).

After Robert Adam's death in 1792, James Adam carried through to completion, sometimes reluctantly, Glasgow works such as the Infirmary, where the brothers had put in proposals at no profit because Robert 'was keen to have the job for fear of its being spoilt'. A scheme of pedimented, four-storey tenement blocks built speculatively by the University on High Street, flanking College Street (built 1793) was probably designed by James Adam. Some of the brothers' schemes were unrealised or scaled down, but they had planted the seeds of monumental grandeur in Glasgow public architecture. Involved in some of the Adams' projects, in all likelihood, as an assistant, was the young David Hamilton, soon to become a dominant figure in the eclectic classical development of central Glasgow in the early nineteenth century.

ROBERT ADAM

Robert Adam [50], although the first of the 'personality' architects, was no isolated genius. Born in 1728, he was brought up in the heart of the Edinburgh architectural establishment. The profits of his father's industrial and contracting work left him, like his brothers and sisters, very rich. By the 1750s Robert, alongside his brother John, had become one of the most prominent architects in Scotland, but the ambition of the self-styled 'British Boy' was to put his business on a UK-wide footing. Adam therefore decided to equip himself for this project by taking the 'Grand Tour' between 1754 and 1757 in pursuit of 'the Antique, the Noble & the Stupendous'. The climax of Adam's tour was a trip across the Adriatic to make drawings of the Roman palace at Spalato (Split), in Croatia. While in Rome, he cultivated friendships and links which would enable him to develop new strengths: Charles-Louis Clerisseau familiarised him with French standards of decorative refinement; Jean-Baptiste Lallemand trained him in landscape painting; while the imaginative genius of Gian Battista Piranesi provided a vision of Roman grandeur to complement Adam's own evolving sensibilities.

For Adam, the point of travelling to Italy was not to be instructed in the 'rules' of classical architecture but to be inspired by its ruins. His ideas formed part of the new tendency towards an emotional response to the world in general, and to antique remains in particular. Both natural and artificial forms could be described as 'Sublime' or 'Picturesque'. These concepts were profoundly shaped by contemporary developments

**[50] James Tassie: 'Robert Adam'
(c.1773)**

The new view of antiquity and individualism was powerfully developed by Robert Adam. He reformulated the 'antique' into a tradition of Scottish romantic classicism which would endure for the

next century and a half, in the work of W.H. Playfair, Alexander Thomson and beyond. Adam's architectural ideas were intermediate between the classical 18th century and the eclectic 19th century. In his classical work, he developed, out of different sources, a recognisable personal 'style' which could be modified to different purposes. The effect of Robert Adam's ideas was also to begin the break-up of architecture into competing types, not least by designing new country houses as 'castles'. Adam's patronage, too, was caught between the 18th and 19th centuries: where the first part of his career was dominated by the country and town houses of the Scottish and English landed classes, after the 1770s he showed a growing concern with design of monumental public buildings in Scotland.

in literature and landscape painting. Adam's own 'picturesque' was conceived in terms of sharp contrasts between 'Architectonick' order and wild romanticism. Clearly, Adam was stirred by the 'terrible' aspect of antique monumentality.

Having completed his Italian stay, Robert Adam moved (in 1758) to England, largely working from London for the next fifteen years and practising jointly with his brother, James. At that date, a move to London was inevitable for a young architect of Robert's ambition, given the huge imbalance in the 1750s between continuing economic uncertainty at home and the showy wealth of the London élite. In 1764, Adam published the drawings of Spalato (with perspectives by Clerisseau), in order 'to introduce me into England with uncommon splendour'.

Although, in 1761, Adam was appointed jointly with William Chambers to the post of Surveyor to the King, very little public work came of this. This posed a potential problem. As Robert and James made clear in their published works, while houses offered ample scope for 'elegance and delicacy of … ornamental decorating', they lacked, in the Adams' view, the 'real greatness' of public buildings, because 'the frequent, but necessary, repetition of windows in private houses, cuts the façade into minute parts'. As a result, much of their domestic work tends to an often misunderstood monumentality.

The 'age of Adam' witnessed the creation of an architectural 'establishment' style which was practised by architects over the next thirty years, recalling something of the pervasive influence of Sir James Murray two hundred years previously. The Adam style lasted well into the nineteenth century, when it was sterilised through its adoption as the official government manner, adopted by Sir Robert Reid at Parliament Square and elsewhere.

NEW ROMANTIC CASTLES

It was James MacPherson's *Ossian* poems, above all, which fixed the principles which would later guide the spread of romantic nationalism across modernising Europe and North America. The importance of James MacPherson's 'discovery' of Ossianic poetry for all branches of Scottish culture in the eighteenth and nineteenth centuries can hardly be overstated. The sudden

**[51] Gosford, East Lothian
(1790–1803), later altered**

The greatest of Robert Adam's classical house designs in Scotland was Gosford, commissioned in 1790 by the 7th Earl of Wemyss. Gosford, in its magnificent Forth-side setting, was clearly intended to evoke the majesty of Spalato, the marine palace of a Roman emperor. Its main (west)

façade was treated as an uncompromising rectangular block, with a central Corinthian-columned portico flanked by pilasters and with an arched Venetian window in each bay. Inside, the three main rooms, forming a vista of 136 ft, were each lit by one of these arched windows.

conceptual transformation of the 'desert' or 'wilderness' of the Highlands' rocky landscape to the setting for the deeds of this first romantic hero had a profound effect on architecture. When Sir James Clerk commissioned the artist Alexander Runciman to decorate the ceiling of the Saloon at Penicuik, he originally requested grotesques in the 'Baths of Titus' style. Then, changing his mind, he renamed the room the 'Hall of Ossian', and asked Runciman to decorate it with Ossianic themes, still in a classical style. General William Gordon, laird of Fyvie, later extended Fyvie c.1790 by building a large new tower (the Gordon Tower) in a style fairly accurately matching Seton's work. This was a crucial departure after a century of classical 'refinement'.

A century after Thirlestane, new, symmetrical castles were built: the most significant by Robert Adam. His castles were the most obvious result of his turn, in the mid-1770s, towards a more assertively picturesque and romantic manner. And they were a sign of the refocusing of his attention back towards Scotland, spurred by the country's accelerating economic recovery, as well as to the well-established international landscape movement exemplified in the work of the painters Claude and Poussin, whose paintings were then arriving in Britain 'by the shipload'.

The first response of Adam to the Scottish landscape movement was to paint and draw romantic castles in a wild setting. Then, from around 1770, beginning at Wedderburn, Adam began to design new country houses in the form of 'castles'. The most obvious and recent precedents for castellated designs were Inveraray, and John Adam's Douglas Castle, but another influence was that of the castellated palaces and houses of the Scottish Renaissance. Adam had worked at a key Scottish building of the earlier 'revival' – Thirlestane – and he came close to the much later concern with accurate 'recording' of the Baronial at Cluny in Aberdeenshire [52]. There was also, from the beginning, a considerable overlap between Adam's castles and elements of his classical house architecture, including not only the general principle of symmetry and interior classicism, but also more specific external features of the classical houses: for example, the massive twin-tower gateway on the south front of Luton Park.

[52] **Robert Adam: view of Cluny Castle**
Note the close similarity with the view published in MacGibbon & Ross [84].

The castellated house designs built by Robert (and James) Adam fell into two phases. The first was a group of relatively plain, rectangular designs. These included Mellerstain, c.1770–8 (a new block, with refined classical interiors, built to link existing wings); the bow-fronted, turreted Wedderburn (1771–5) and the plainer Caldwell (1773–4). However, from the mid-1770s, there began a series of much more romantic compositions. These exploited the play of light and shade, with the boldly geometrical shapes of towers and turrets. This second group began with an unbuilt scheme of 1774 for the 3rd Earl of Rosebery, which proposed the transformation of the 'L'-shaped tower-house of Barnbougle Castle into a splay-planned block with bastion-like courtyard. In these turreted, triangular forms, there was a striking overlap with classical house design, including both his father's Minto and the neo-classical geometry of his own Walkinshaw. A slightly later splay-plan castellated design, also unexecuted, was that for Beauly Castle (1777). Castles which were actually built in this

**[53] Culzean Castle, Ayrshire
(1777–92)**

It was at the 'whimsical but magnificent Castle of Colane' (in the words of Clerk of Penicuik, in 1788), that Adam's patron, the 10th Earl of Cassilis, a lawyer and MP, encouraged the architect to 'indulge to the utmost his romantic genius'. Adam added to Culzean, already enlarged in 1777, a new block containing a circular saloon, library and bedroom suite, and hollowed out an elliptical staircase inside the original section. The house was reached by a new landscaped approach across the designed 'ruin' of a causeway.

manner included Culzean [**53**] (from 1777; north elevation from 1785); Oxenfoord (1780–2); Dalquharran (from 1782, and extended 1880 to its present length); Pitfour (*c.*1785); Seton (1790), which echoed the rippling attached towers of Bruce's Thirlestane; Airthrey (from 1790); and Stobs (1792–3). In all these cases, severe, tower-like blocks with unadorned, almost neo-classical fenestration were arranged in symmetrical clusters and plan-forms which were designed to be suitable for axial views, but, at the same time, to 'read' asymmetrically when seen in landscape. Another significant unexecuted castellated design was that for Fullarton (1790).

We began this chapter with the neo-Baronial of Sir William Bruce at Thirlestane, only to see the value system that produced it completely overturned by the very same architect. Bruce is said to have 'restored' classical architecture, and we saw how its ever stricter rules were undermined by Robert Adam, who again looked to the past to create his stunning series of set-piece castles. We close with Culzean: the Romantic bookends of eighteenth-century Scottish architecture.

[**54**] **Daniel Robertson:**
design for a gate lodge (*c.*1800)

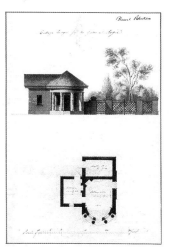

The end of the 18th century also saw another response to Romantic ideas and landscape in domestic architecture: the 'primitive' artistic cottage. Eighteenth-century architectural theorists had become interested in the origins of architecture. The idea of the first man, Adam, as the 'first architect' in his 'primitive hut' had huge appeal. Examples of this type of thatched-roof dwelling are to be found throughout Robert Adam's drawings (Daniel Robertson is thought to be a relation of Adam's). The pioneering built example was by John Clerk of Eldin in the grounds of Eldin House, Lasswade (1769–74), a summerhouse with ingleneuk chimney and turf roof, ambiguously nicknamed 'Adam's Hut' after his brother-in-law, Robert.

[55] Port Dundas Canal Offices, Glasgow (1812)

[56] Main entrance to Melrose Station (1847–9)

The new eclecticism allowed new building types to be made to 'match' their surroundings. The offices of the Port Dundas Canal, 1812, resembled a villa, but by 1847, John Miller's design for Melrose Station imitated a miniature Jacobean country house, in deference to nearby Abbotsford.

Previously, classicism had been perceived as a set of rules, but Robert Adam had 'broken' these rules, creating a personal style. The way was now clear for the development of competing styles. The great theme of nineteenth-century architecture was eclecticism: the licence to design in a multitude of styles, for a multitude of new buildings: libraries, museums, prisons, courthouses, banks, insurance offices, or shops – all in search of an image. Thus was born the crucial idea that a building's appearance could somehow define or promote the values historically associated with that appearance. Sir Walter Scott's gas lighting and up-to-the-minute service arrangements at Abbotsford could all be framed within an image of 'oldness'.

Scott's Romanticism was part of a Europe-wide repudiation of rationalism as a guiding principle. In such a movement, the appreciation of 'untamed' nature was crucial. In cities all over Europe, Classicism and Romanticism were dramatically linked, but the most spectacular example was Edinburgh. Here, geography and history combined in the creation of the world's first 'Sublime' city. By the 1820s, Edinburgh had already been dubbed 'The Athens of the North': as much a comment on the city's literary achievements as its appearance. Now, Edinburgh styled itself an Athenian 'city of virtue' to London's 'commercial', Imperial Rome. In 1829, T.H. Shepherd's publication, *Modern Athens*, reinforced the concept and the city pushed ahead with its programme of classical and non-classical buildings: temples and spires; monumental compositions and vistas. In Glasgow, later expansion was even more ambitious. Where Edinburgh remained a city of controlled views – summed up in *Modern Athens* – Glasgow planned in an open-ended way, creating romantic classical buildings of great intensity, including Alexander Thomson's series of city churches.

Along with the expansion of cities came a new definition of landscape as the setting for the romantic adventure of Scotch Baronial architecture. Robert Adam's experiments in castle building were taken forward in an astonishing series of set-piece Baronial compositions from the Borders to the Highlands. Along with this new presentation of Highland imagery came the final, often brutal, phase of rural 'improvement' in the Clearances, carried through by a new class of middle men, such as Robert Adam's own nephew, James Loch.

ROMANTIC EDINBURGH AND THE CITY AS MONUMENT

In the early part of the nineteenth century, modern cities adopted the architecture of Ancient Greece, as a style for 'national' buildings, particularly assemblies with their democratic overtones. In Scotland, images of Greek antiquity were especially significant in the 'North British' era when Edinburgh was keen to cast itself in the role of philosophical 'think tank' for the new Britain. When a national monument to the Napoleonic war dead was proposed for Edinburgh's Calton Hill, it was quickly decided that it should be a 'facsimile of the Parthenon'. In 1822, the English architect–archaeologist C.R. Cockerell drew up the designs, which were then (partly) completed under the supervision of W.H. Playfair. However this phase of replication, informed by measured studies of Greek monuments, was short-lived in Edinburgh and elsewhere. A new phase of Graecomania soon began, which captured the spirit, rather than the detail, of Greece. Also, once the Greek had been packaged and presented, it left the way open for other styles which were vigorously taken up after the 1820s. By the 1830s, Grecian public institutions were built alongside Roman banks, Baroque churches and Gothic monumental spires.

[57] Aerial view of Woodlands Hill, Glasgow (from 1854)

Eclecticism allowed a differentiation between buildings and areas within the mid-19th century city. In the planning of Glasgow Town Council's private development at Woodlands Hill, the architect Charles Wilson used varying styles. In its residential buildings, a palazzo style was used for the inward-looking Park Circus, but a more flamboyant, high-roofed French Renaissance for the outward-facing Park Terrace. At the Free Church College (from 1856) the architect created a great triple-towered city monument which 'addressed' the whole city. Although piecemeal, including the early 'boulevard' of Sauchiehall Street, the area was conceived as a single entity, not a collection of stand-alone monuments. This compositional grouping extends also to the 'natural' forms of Kelvin- grove. We can see this even within the scope of one key house, at No.22 Park Circus, which is something of an inner/outer ring hybrid, its first floor oriel on the side elevation allowing a view southwards over the park.

[58] William Stark: Justiciary Court, Saltmarket, Glasgow (1809–14), later remodelled

The driving force of Grecian classicism in Scotland was a reaction against Robert Adam's 'profusion of embellishment' towards more severe forms. The architect who introduced these revolutionary tendencies was William Stark, whom we find in St Petersburg in 1798 – one of the great centres of European neo-classicism – but home in Scotland again by 1803, where he designed the rationally-planned Hunterian Museum at Glasgow University (1804–5). The breakthrough for the Greek Revival came at Stark's Justiciary Court House (built 1809–14; rebuilt 1913) in Glasgow: a French neo-classical horizontality was combined with a huge Greek Doric portico for the first time in Scotland [58]. However, Stark's work was really more concerned with the interplay of forms than the application of detail. St George's Tron Church, Glasgow (1807–8) allows two such contradictory shapes (a triumphal-arch fronted block like Adam's University, and a soaring tower) to come together. Stark was also capable of producing stunning interiors, such as the Advocates' (now Upper) Library, a domed hall of Corinthian columns in Parliament Square, Edinburgh. Just before his death, Stark moved to Edinburgh, where his most immediate legacy emerged in the work of his pupil, William Playfair.

The best example of the 'city as monument' tendency is a group of Edinburgh buildings created over thirty years. In 1839, the spired Tolbooth St John Church was begun by James Gillespie Graham at the head of the vista up the Mound. Then, in 1843, came the Disruption of the Established Church of Scotland, and the founding of the rival Free Church of Scotland, who sited their New College at the top of the Mound, directly in front of the Tolbooth Church. W.H. Playfair did not

W. H. Playfair (1790–1857)

W.H. Playfair [74] was a well-connected establishment figure, whose career began in the office of William Stark. In 1816 he toured France, seemingly the first Scottish architect to examine Napoleonic architecture first-hand. In 1815 he had won the competition to complete Adam's unfinished Edinburgh University (1819–27), proposing the exact completion of Adam's east façade. His own contributions to the complex were the provision of monumental interior spaces, including the museum and Upper Library.

Playfair's transition to Greek neo-classicism took place in 1818–20, at Dollar Academy, in a Sublime landscape setting. The Academy's main façade comprised a Doric portico with flanking pavilions. In 1822 he began two important neo-Grecian commissions, this time in Edinburgh. The first was the Royal Institution, which Playfair designed and further enlarged in 1832–5 to provide exhibition spaces for manufactures. The same year the building of the National Monument began. Although the money ran out and the scheme was abandoned, the National Monument promoted an exceptionally strong theme in Scottish culture – the 'cult of the dead'. At this stage the expression of collective sentiment was still channelled through classicism: the association with a rough hewn, 'national' style had not been made.

From the late 1820s, Playfair continued to build in a monumental neo-Greek mode, as at the Edinburgh Surgeons' Hall (1829–32). However, his most powerful contribution to Edinburgh's romantic urbanism was made through a return to a Baroque grandeur: St Stephen's Church, 1827–8 [59]. Here, Playfair used the pattern

of podium-like pavilions to accommodate the church, fronted with an enormous tower, blocklike and sepulchral in character. This 'romanticising' of the Grecian through essentially skyline features was widely prevalent at the time.

[59] St Stephen's Church, Edinburgh (1827–8)

[60] Thomas Hamilton: Old Royal
High School, Edinburgh (1825–9)
(seen from Salisbury Crags)

[61] St Bernard's Crescent,
Edinburgh (from 1824)

*The most monumental Greek street
architecture was St Bernard's Crescent,
one of a group designed by James
Milne in 1824. This fairly ordinary
row of dwellings was fronted with a
massive array of two-storey Doric
columns. The residents seem barely to
have room to squeeze into their homes.*

block the view of the church, instead, he audaciously 'captured' its steeple in the frame of the new College's towers, when seen above his Royal Institution building. To complete the grouping on the Mound, Playfair was asked in 1849 by the Board of Manufacturers to prepare designs for the twin National Gallery and Royal Scottish Academy. In response to criticisms that no building should be erected on this sensitive location, Playfair described it as 'being like the hub of a wheel, the centre-point of the great cyclorama of North Edinburgh'. Clearly, no Modern Athenian building was to be designed in isolation.

Playfair's main rival in Edinburgh was an architect of a quite different sort. The son of a mason, Thomas Hamilton had architectural talent that was quickly recognised in the meritocracy of the early nineteenth-century town. Hamilton's first breakthrough, however, came in the west, where he designed another important example of the classical national memorial genre: the earliest of the Burns monuments, put up in 1820–3 at the poet's birthplace, Alloway (near Ayr), only twenty-five years after his death.

On Calton Hill Thomas Hamilton designed what was, perhaps, the single most significant single monument of Edinburgh classical romanticism: the Royal High School (1825–9) [60]. The building was originally envisaged as a very square, pilastered composition on a podium at St James's Square, based on the model of the Theseion. For the building's eventual, rocky site, Hamilton evolved (from 1825) a far looser vision, presenting the small group of buildings as a multi-level temple structure.

EDINBURGH NEW TOWN

The conformity of the expanded New Town – whose population rose from around 15,000 to 40,000 in the first quarter of the century – was the result not of public regulation but of private mechanisms. The houses were built by speculators working according to designs specified by the private owners of the land in their feuing conditions. Architecturally, there was a move from Adamesque Roman to Greek, and in layout, James Craig's earlier grid was rejected in favour of designed irregularity and greenery.

The development of the Mound complex to further link the Old and New Towns in the late 1840s and 1850s signalled the end of Edinburgh's 'romantic' or 'national' classicism. Already, by then, 'Modern Athens' was over – brought to an end by the bankruptcy of the Town Council in 1833 over the Leith Docks extension. But the spirit of improvement had already spread throughout Scotland.

[62] Aerial view of the north-western New Town, Edinburgh (from 1820s)

In proposals of 1813 for an extension of the New Town on part of Calton Hill, William Stark led the way in attempting to make clear differentiations in residential schemes, advocating a combination of convenience and landscaped effect. Playfair backed this up in a report of 1819, blasting the 'complete uniformity' seen in 'many parts of the New Town of Edinburgh'. He proposed a vast 'new Town between Edinburgh and Leith' with a radial layout, square and terraces around Calton Hill.

The trend towards a looser residential pattern in the New Town reached its climax in the development of the Earl of Moray's Drumsheugh estate. The centrepiece of this development, Moray Place (1822–36, designed by Gillespie Graham; centre) was a massive space, ringed by ranks of giant orders. We can contrast this 'closed' formality with Playfair's 'open', landscape orientated Royal Circus (1821–3; top left). On the ground at Royal Circus, the two matching crescents are so far apart and interrupted by planting as to appear almost unrelated.

[63] **Castle St, Aberdeen (from 1801)**

Aberdeen granite was previously considered too hard for decorative work but the Greek Revival offered the chance to bring out its icy precision. The city's first finely constructed granite building, James Burn's Aberdeen Banking Company office in Castle Street, was built in 1801–2. By the 1830s, the cutting of granite was revolutionised by the introduction of steam-powered technology. The north-eastern granite industry expanded and even began an export drive.

[64] Archibald Simpson (1790–1847)

Archibald Simpson was the main rival of Aberdeen City Architect, John Smith, architect of the refined classical screen to St Nicholas's churchyard (1829). In 1813, Simpson began a series of largely Grecian public buildings, beginning with the Ionic-porticoed Medico-Chirugical Society's Hall, King Street (1818), and the similarly porticoed Assembly Rooms (1820–2). Simpson's Athenaeum (or Union Buildings), 1822–3, was a simplified version of the Robert Adam multi-level idea; its great Ionic-porticoed entrance front rhetorically addressed the square around the Mercat Cross. Elsewhere in the city, the colossal façade of the New Market (1840–2) brought shopping under cover for the first (but certainly not the last) time in the city. The need to build churches in a hurry applied dramatically, of course, to the Free Church. Archibald Simpson's 'Triple Kirks' (1843), a Marburg-spired complex of largely brick buildings, seen here in the background, was built in a matter of weeks to house three congregations displaced from St Nicholas's Kirk.

In Aberdeen, there was a series of bold schemes more or less following the earlier Edinburgh models of axes and 'bridge streets'. The most celebrated scheme was an 1801–5 scheme for a new, axial route running south-west from the old centre for a mile: Union Street. The centrepiece was a bridge at the Denburn designed by Thomas Fletcher and Thomas Telford. In contrast to Edinburgh's South Bridge, all old buildings in its path were demolished.

THE RISE OF GLASGOW

In the first quarter of the nineteenth century, Glasgow was growing faster than any other city in Europe. The city began its attempts to marshal this growth through increasing municipal interventions, such as street lighting, introduced as early as 1818. However, there was not yet a policy of area redevelopment, and the period of civic triumph was also one of crises. The city was racked by violent disturbances, culminating in the 1819–20 insurrection by handloom weavers. Solutions focused on attempts to control the 'mob', but alongside these were socio-evangelical attempts to create a 'godly commonwealth' uniting all classes. Already, Glasgow's culture of reform and religion was emerging.

For the wealthy, the first instinct was escape. In Laurieston on the south bank of the Clyde, Peter Nicholson designed Carlton Place, the city's first two unified classical residential row façades in the Charlotte Square manner (built in 1802–4

[65] The Necropolis, Glasgow (from 1833)

David Hamilton also introduced architecture to an early 'park' cemetery, the Glasgow Necropolis, dramatically situated on a hill behind the Cathedral. The layout was based on the Père Lachaise cemetery in Paris. A walk among the monuments was designed to 'banish preternatural fears'. Hamilton's works here included the gateway (1833), lodge (1839–40), and 'Bridge of Sighs' (1833–4) over which the remains of Glasgow's ruling classes were conveyed by four 'mutes' to their last, architect-designed, resting places.

[66] Free Church College, Glasgow (1856–61)

The late work of David Hamilton was highly influential among younger architects, especially Charles Wilson, Hamilton's former pupil and assistant (from 1827–37). Wilson was an important figure in the mid-19th century. His greatest work was the Free Church College on Woodlands Hill. Like Playfair's Mound grouping in Edinburgh, Woodlands Hill was the scenic centrepiece of the new, mid-century Glasgow, and the College was its crowning element. Its design also set out to broadcast the power and authority of the Free Church through a tall towered silhouette, but in an open, Glasgow fashion, visible from all directions. All three towers are massive yet attenuated, with slit-like patterning, giving this classical complex a strongly Romantic character. This was a character – if not a style – that was to be invested with an astonishing emotional intensity by Wilson's contemporary, Alexander Thomson.

David Hamilton (1768–1843)

The most influential Glasgow architect of the first half of the nineteenth century was David Hamilton. Hamilton (no relation of his Edinburgh namesake Thomas), a former employee of Robert Adam, often collaborated with Glasgow's Superintendent of Public Works, James Cleland, who was directly responsible for a number of public buildings and monuments. He organised the paid attraction of Glasgow Green as a civic park in 1815, where he had already commissioned Hamilton to design a Nelson Monument in the form of an obelisk.

Hamilton's early public buildings combined a taste for architectural complexity with a concern for skyline impact inherited from the Adams. A series of public buildings with tall spires in the tolbooth/town house manner included Hutcheson's Hospital (1802–5) and Port Glasgow Town Buildings (1815–16). From the late 1820s, however, he used a far more florid architectural treatment, combined with a new urbanism. The key example was the Royal Exchange (1827–9), where he re-fronted the Cunninghame Mansion of 1778–80 with a rich Greek Corinthian portico. The Exchange also closed the vista down Ingram Street and created a new civic space.

and 1813–18). Then there was a move out to new western suburbs, with the feuing out of the Blythswood estate, which was built up from 1816. Blythswood Square was laid out from 1823 to 1829, possibly to the designs of William Burn or George Smith, and executed by John Brash. By this time, Glasgow had begun to assume the mixed layout of a capitalist city. The original eighteenth-century extension area became transformed into a centre of commerce and public monuments.

ALEXANDER THOMSON

Inseparable from the story of Glasgow is its greatest nineteenth century architect: Alexander Thomson (1817–75). Trained by Robert Foote (to 1836) and John Baird I, Thomson began his independent career in 1847, when he joined another (unrelated) John Baird. His work from that point accommodated the commercial, spiritual and social needs of booming Glasgow:

speculative offices and chambers, churches, tenements, suburban and marine villas.

It is tempting to put Thomson in a special category of world 'greats', like Robert Adam, but this would be to miss the point. Undoubtedly, the seeds of Thomson's Sublime classicism were sown by Adam and brought to flower by David Hamilton [65] and William Stark. The crucial new ingredient was religion. Although completely locked into the circumstances of his day as a property speculator and developer, Thomson's great-grandfather had been a Covenanter, and he was an elder of one of his own churches (Caledonia Road). Underpinning everything was his belief that 'Religion has been the soul of art from the beginning'.

The idea of architecture ideally having an 'eternal' quality had been something of a commonplace in European architecture. For example, Christopher Wren had written that

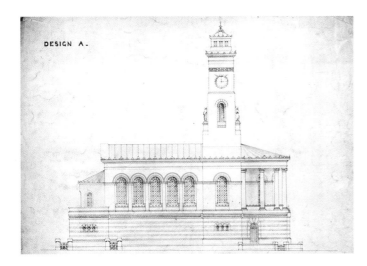

[67] Charles Wilson: unbuilt design for Kelvinside Parish Church, Glasgow (1858)

There are clear similarities with Thomson in the great podium and pseudo-temple formula. The obvious difference is in the use of arched construction.

[68] St Vincent St Church, Glasgow (1857–9)

In 1856, Thomson formed a partner-ship with his brother George, a Christian businessman who later gave up architecture to become a missionary. One of the first commissions of A. and G. Thomson was the building of St Vincent Street United Presbyterian (1857–9). Here, the Glasgow interaction between religion and capitalism was explicit. The Gordon Street church where George Thomson worshipped suddenly found that the rise in land values had left them with a considera-

ble asset. They decided to realise this by moving to a new site further out in Blythswood. The Thomson brothers bought the old site and erected the Grosvenor Building on it (1859–61), while in their capacity as architects, they designed the congregation's new St Vincent Street church, along with a tenement next door to it, in order to maximise rental value. St Vincent Street's sharply sloping site, most frequently seen from below, offered the opportunity to design a building which exceeded in monumentality even Playfair's St Stephen's. The composition comprises two elements: a main church block conceived as a mound-like structure of interpenetrating temple, lower 'aisles' and pylons, on an exaggeratedly tall podium; and a huge steeple which appears like a solid obelisk of stone, topped by a fantastic conglomeration of Egyptian and oriental detail. It seems likely that the high podium was intended to recall the Temple of Solomon. Inside,

the furniture and fittings, all designed personally by Thomson, echoed the external emphasis on mass, with its heavy single-piece pews, exploiting the machine-assembly techniques of shipbuilding, and a pulpit that is almost a building in its own right, with a theatrical concealed entrance allowing the minister to appear, without ceremony, in the middle of the auditorium. The scheme was completed by stencilled decoration in primary 'archaeological' Grecian colours.

'Building certainly ought to have the Attribute of the eternal, and therefore the only Thing uncapable of new Fashions.' However, this idea was powerfully charged by Thomson with a new intensity [colour plate 19]. For Thomson, probably also influenced by Masonic philosophy, the beginning of architecture lay in Ancient Egypt, whose mass and repetition represented the 'endeavour to realise the idea of eternity'. The imagined architecture of the Old Testament, including Solomon's Temple, was held by Thomson to have possessed this quality.

His structural logic and proportional discipline had strong mystic overtones which developed throughout his career. For Thomson, the role of architectural grandeur was to provide communication with God, through its ability to carry the mind 'away into space'. He believed that aspects of Early Christian architecture anticipated the Presbyterian 'preaching box'. However, he also argued that the arch was 'a bricklayer's contrivance' and that the Romans had 'littered Europe' with ruins as a result of its use. The Italian round arches of his early villas were abandoned from the early 1850s, and 1856 saw his first large church commission, Caledonia Road.

THOMSON'S CHURCHES

The church building of the mid-century was dominated by the activity of the three Presbyterian groupings – the Established Church, the Free Church, and Thomson's church, the United Presbyterians – although the revival of Catholicism and Episcopalianism would eventually challenge that dominance. For all denominations, as the cities grew, the main concern was to build quickly.

The apparently obvious style for churches was Gothic, but in fact the most important developments stemmed chiefly from the dynamic classicism of Stark and Playfair, above all, St Stephen's Church which we looked at in its proper context as a city monument. The rightful heir of St Stephen's is St George's Free Church, Shandwick Place, Edinburgh (1867–9), a sumptuously Corinthian-columned building by David Bryce, whose complex tower remained unbuilt.

In the west, there was a far more forceful development of this ecclesiastical classicism, led by Alexander Thomson. The first of his three major churches was Caledonia Road United Presbyterian (1856–7). Here the 'portico and podium' arrangement of Playfair's Surgeons' Hall was combined with an Italianate tower similar to Wilson's campanile at the Free Church College on Woodlands Hill. Like Wilson, too, is the insistence on townscape through the integration with new adjoining tenement blocks. Inside, Thomson introduced vivid coloured decoration for the first time in United Presbyterian churches.

In Thomson's final large church, Queen's Park United Presbyterian (1867–9), the site was flat and uninspiring. As at Caledonia Road, Thomson therefore placed the 'portico' on a high podium to give the design monumental presence. The entrance was sited to one side of a pilastered screen defining the awkward boundary and the lower adjacent halls, which formed a base for the symmetrical upper work. Here, the detailing seems to have come out of some biblical illustration or Egypto-Babylonian dream architecture of endless compressed colonnades.

Inside Queen's Park Church, Thomson's experiments in polychromatic decoration were taken a stage further, with the artist Daniel Cottier, who was working at that time with William Leiper in the design of a neo-Gothic church at Dowanhill. Cottier, trained in stained glass design in Glasgow, was a remarkable designer whose early interior schemes took the rationalist ideas of the Edinburgh designer D.R. Hay in new directions. At Queen's Park, for example, primary colours were abandoned for a more complex framework of tertiary blues and reds – an aspect of the later nineteenth-century avant-garde rejection of vivid colour for more muted 'artistic' design. Cottier moved to London in 1869, and subsequently on to the United States; by 1873 his decorative-art and art-dealing business was disseminating 'artistic' taste across the anglophone world, with branches in New York, London and Sydney.

PLANNING FOR 'ETERNITY'

With the outward expansion of the city, the question arose of what to do with the old, now decaying core around Glasgow Cross. A controversial new type of 'improvement' was initiated: area clearance and redevelopment. As Glasgow's population spiralled, 'improvement' was now taken on as an urban

[69] Peddie & Kinnear: Drumsheugh Gardens, Edinburgh (1874)

[70] Walmer Crescent, Glasgow (1857–62)

We can compare Peddie and Kinnear's beautifully designed and executed composition of terraced houses at Drumsheugh Gardens in the western New Town of Edinburgh with Thomson's Walmer Crescent in Glasgow. Although Walmer Crescent was described – rather archaically at this date – as being 'occupied exclusively by rich merchants', it was in fact a tenement block, and here we come to the question of the architectural 'treatment' of this building type. By the mid-century, Edinburgh New Town had more flatted or 'doubled' dwellings than it did vertically stacked housing. Were these fit for the new urban middle classes or not? Very often, tenements fronted main roads or formed the centre or end blocks of larger buildings, but there had been continuing worries over their status, even from the late 18th century when Edinburgh Town Council had rejected houses 'set in flats' for Charlotte Square. William Burn's Henderson Row (1829) was a tenement masquerading, through its use of porticoed main-door flats, as a line of

row houses. Architecturally, indeed, there were many links with middle-class terraces of individual dwellings, but the overall aesthetic seemed to have remained closer to neo-classical uniformity and severity. Architectural embellishment tended to be graded on a scale with status. In contrast with European tenements, the use of fine ashlar construction in this way set Scottish tenements apart.

[71] Alexander Thomson: Egyptian Halls, Union Street, Glasgow (1871–3)

necessity. At first this was still not about dealing with poverty, but rather the forcible removal of the poor from their decayed housing. Rapidly, however, improvement took on a strongly religious overtone as Glasgow took over Edinburgh's 'city of classical virtue' idea, transforming it into a drive towards the creation of a city of God.

In 1866, the Town Council set up a Trust to acquire and re-develop an area centred on Glasgow Cross. In contrast to the romantic, scenographic ideas which influenced Edinburgh's redevelopment ideas, Glasgow's were uncompromisingly rational. They admired Haussmann's replanning of Paris in 1853–69 by the creation of new boulevards. Provost John Blackie headed an 1866 delegation to visit Haussmann's 'great works'; Glasgow was to become a 'second Paris'.

In the field of middle-class housing, the 1830s saw the first breaks from grid patterns. These included George Smith's Woodside Crescent, Terrace and Place (from 1831 to the mid-1840s) and Alexander Taylor's Royal Terrace (1839–49). These developments carried forward Edinburgh terrace designs of the mid-1820s, which had shown how the individual house or tenement unit could be presented as one architectural unit. However, two major initiatives offered the Glaswegian alternative of dynamic openness: Woodlands Hill and Great Western Road.

We have already looked at the plans by Charles Wilson for Park Circus and Terrace; these formed part of a politically contentious overall plan for the area which Wilson prepared for the Town Council in 1854, including a dramatically contoured new park. Great Western Road was a more ambitious undertaking, its aim to facilitate the development of a new, select suburb on the Kelvinside estate, which was not yet part of municipal Glasgow. This boulevard was itself to be lined with terraced developments in an assortment of classical styles. Wilson's Roman Renaissance Kirklee Terrace of 1845 was first and the climax was reached at Alexander Thomson's highly restrained Great Western Terrace (from 1869). Thomson's block recalled the simplified Grecian of Thomas Hamilton's Royal High School, which Thomson admired.

In the south of the city, Thomson's 1–10 Moray Place (from 1859) used rigid horizontal repetition to provide an answer to the visual 'problem' of intrusive fenestration posed by Adam. Thomson's Walmer Crescent (1857–62) [70], built in isolation adjoining Paisley Road West, was composed in masses – great solids – rather than framed by orders.

The relentless march of stone as the prestige Scottish building material met an obstacle in Glasgow in the 1850s. The threat came from an attempt to exploit the possibilities of iron construction in city-centre warehouses. John Baird I's Gardner's warehouse (1855–6) for the first time used an exposed iron frame, offering almost uninterrupted glazing. What now would be the status of stone when iron seemed to offer instant architecture? For a variety of reasons, instead of diminishing, stone seemed to take on a new prestige. At John Honeyman's Ca d'Oro of 1872, the Venetian theme of Gardner's warehouse was taken up, but already there had been a reaction away from exposed iron towards hybrid forms: Honeyman's design combined a masonry 'frame' with cast iron bays, painted to resemble stone. So why did iron architecture, rather than construction, falter? The reason was partly safety: extreme heat would cause an iron-framed building to buckle and collapse, so steps had to be taken to protect the material from fire. The main department store of Wylie & Lochhead was rebuilt by James Sellars in fire-proof form following a fire which destroyed a cast-iron structure: its iron frontage and tall shopping hall was sleeved in terracotta. The other reason for a reluctance to 'express' iron architecturally perhaps goes deeper. Alexander Thomson again provides the answer.

Thomson's Buck's Head building in Argyle Street (1862–3) was a hybrid arrangement of cast-iron and stone, but his growing insistence on the 'eternal' properties of masonry construction led to his complete rejection of externally expressed iron. Other Thomson designs all but concealed the iron structure within a stone monumentality, emphasising post and lintel construction mixed with horizontal repetition in grid-like façades. Key examples were the Grosvenor Building of 1859–61 and Grecian Buildings (1865), a corner block with end pavilions and deeply-recessed top floor behind stumpy columns. But the most powerful of all was Egyptian Halls (1871–3) [71], a four-storey block designed, horizontally, in accordance with 'the principle of repetition'.

The Country House and the Villa

By 1800, the landed classes emerged from a century of improvement richer than ever, and the building of country houses expanded. However, the typical classical country house set in an informal landscape was going out of fashion, as the landed classes began to favour more romantic, irregular compositions. But the last of the great classical houses was also the greatest.

Already a big house, Hamilton Palace was stupendously enlarged in 1822–6 by Alexander, 10th Duke of Hamilton, a man of continental tastes and ambitions [72]. Before even succeeding to the dukedom in 1819, he had commissioned designs in autocratic style from Giacomo Quarenghi, then imperial Russian architect. In 1843, 'Il Magnifico' (as he was nicknamed) married his heir into the French imperial family. More importantly, Hamilton was one of the world's richest men.

In 1819 Hamilton commissioned grandiose new designs from Francesco Saponieri, before engaging David Hamilton, who enlarged Saponieri's proposal in 1822. As built, the effect of this vast building with its massive freestanding portico was much more royal palace than ducal residence. Inside, the theme was continued, the entrance hall repeating the rich Corinthian order of the exterior. An expert visitor noted that 'the whole ameublement was on a greater scale of costliness … than I had seen in any other palace.' As a country-house design, Hamilton Palace had very little influence among the aristocracy: it was financially beyond any other patron, but its classical richness was nevertheless influential in smaller urban commissions, particularly banks.

[72] David Hamilton: Hamilton Palace new façade (from 1822)

The difficulty with austere classicism was that it would not easily adapt to the new demand for informality. Nevertheless, William Burn fully developed domestic privacy, at first using a classical language. At Camperdown (designed in 1821 and built 1824–6 for the 2nd Viscount Duncan), Burn placed a separate family wing at right angles and put the main entrance to one side, thereby stressing the 'image' of the house over the way in which it would be used. However, it was not ideal. A new, 'informal' style was needed which did not require the various new functions to be crammed into a classical 'box'.

The leading exponent of informality was W.H. Playfair, with a series of designs in the late 1820s, including Belmont (1828–30), Edinburgh, and Drumbanagher in Ireland (designed 1829). At Dunphail, Morayshire (1828–33), Playfair's tendency to low massiveness, with sweeping eaves, was carried to an extreme. The basic ingredients of the Italianate style were simple, irregular blocks and a tower, or towers: a pattern taken up all over the country. However, a more assertively 'national', stone-built, romantic image was soon wanted. Classical buildings, especially after the publication of Pugin's *Contrasts* which depicted the town as a rationalist nightmare, were now associated with public buildings. Would it now be possible to express national romanticism through architecture? The early nineteenth century viewed this prospect with great excitement. But what should these buildings look like? Britton's *Architectural Antiquities*, from 1805, answered that question in England. Later, the demand for more authentic renderings of the 'national' would lead to the researches of R.W. Billings, and to the eventual emergence of the 'Scotch Baronial'.

As classicism in country-house design for the landed classes lost its appeal, a new building type – the villa – emerged. The smaller villa, as the centrepiece of an estate or as a retreat, had existed since the Renaissance, and had been reinvigorated in the eighteenth century, when its social focus gradually widened from lesser landowners to the professional classes. The early nineteenth century still witnessed the building of small classical dwellings, but now there was even an attempt, such as at Arthur Lodge in Edinburgh (c.1827–30, probably by Thomas Hamilton), to play *down* their scale in order to achieve a more convincingly villa-like effect.

The major growth area in villa building was in a belt around the cities, at first especially Edinburgh. By 1800, Midlothian was studded with the country retreats of the Edinburgh middle classes. In Glasgow [73 & colour plate 18], David Hamilton designed a series of simply-detailed villas on small 'estates' on the outskirts, such as Kilmardinny House (c.1815), Aikenhead (1806, extended 1823) and Camphill (c.1810). Also well underway was the development of marine summer-residences. These were clustered especially on the Clyde. During the years 1820–40 the domination of the symmetrical villa began to be challenged, partly through the influence of the parallel developments in country-house architecture, but chiefly through the rationalising of the limited space available to the villa client or speculator. A more informal, picturesque, asym-

[73] Villa, Pollokshields, Glasgow (early 19th c.)

By the 1820s a new trend towards the establishment of the villa as a principal residence of middle-class owners was taking hold. With improved transport by land and sea, especially through the railways, suburban villas were laid out on increasingly large and regularised patterns of streets, alongside high-class tenements. David Rhind's West Pollokshields, for example, was feued out in 1851. Against the background of otherwise generally plain classical villas, the area also includes a sequence of houses by Alexander Thomson,

ranging from the round-arched Italian manner of 'The Knowe', Albert Drive (from 1852) to the cubic Graeco-Egyptian of 'Ellisland', Nithsdale Road (1871). His 'Maria Villa' at Langside (1856–7) comprised a pair of dwellings on an ingenious interlocked plan. Thomson's earlier villa work, before his repudiation of the round arch, was especially to be found in the burgeoning marine suburbs. Along the Clyde, at Cove and Kilcreggan, Thomson built an earlier and more austere version of The Knowe, at Craig Ailey (1850), sited spectacularly above a rugged cliff, like Adam's Culzean.

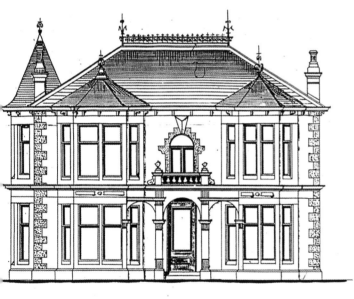

FRONT ELEVATION

BACK ELEVATION

Plan 10 A villa in Pollokshields.

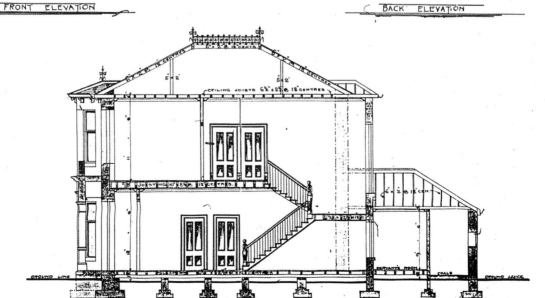

metrical style of villa architecture was well suited to housing the growing 'commercial' class and their attendant solicitors, teachers, doctors and, of course, architects.

DAVID BRYCE AND SCOTCH BARONIAL

Stylistically, Scotch Baronial can be traced back to Robert Adam but, as we have seen, his castles were rooted in a tradition of classical planning. The function of the great country house was changing. Now, families wanted even more privacy, especially from their servants, who had reached a low point in their historical status. Servants' segregation was allied with accessibility to the main quarters, continuing a theme which had been played out during the Bruce years when servants had ceased to be relatives or members of aristocratic families. Externally, architects now looked back to a much earlier period of Scottish architecture for their inspiration. Along with a romantic profile, these new 'castles' allowed the plan to follow the modern needs of the users. The apparent informality of the Baronial as a style offered the chance architecturally to express the building's different functions in a hierarchy of forms, from stable block to main dwelling.

Prior to the publication of R.W. Billings' series, *The Baronial*

and Ecclesiastical Antiquities of Scotland in 1845–52, much of the architecture, like much of the culture, was avowedly 'North British'. The most prominent stylistic trend was that of 'Tudor' or 'Jacobean'. Here some English architects were initially employed: for instance, William Wilkins (at Dalmeny, 1814–17 and Dunmore Park). But it was William Burn who became the key figure. Burn developed the possibilities of his own mixed style of 'Tudorbethan' at Saltoun (1817), Carstairs (1822–4), Blairquhan (1820–4) and Garscube (1826).

More than any other architect, David Bryce [79] is associated with the formulation of the new architecture. Mid-nineteenth century Scotch Baronial formed part of an international movement. Universal 'Italian' styles were rejected in favour of more accurate 'national' styles: for instance, in France, by a 'neo-Renaissance' based on the Loire châteaux. For such a movement, new, national types of source-publications were necessary. Billings provided such a publication. His finished illustrations presented dramatically shaded perspectives of castles and churches. As with Adam, the buildings, even if symmetrical on plan, were presented in an irregular and asymmetrical manner for scenographic effect. Billings' publication became the source book of the Baronial: that is what it was for.

Who were the patrons of this 'national' style? Not exclusively the *nouveaux riches*, as is often assumed. Mid-nineteenth century Baronial works would be commissioned both by the established aristocracy, such as the Duke of Atholl (1869–76 alterations to Blair Castle), and by industrialists such as the Glaswegian chemical giant Charles Tennant (The Glen, 1855–60), who used his country house as a power-base for his political ambitions. The ultimate patron was, of course, the monarch. In this respect, Queen Victoria's purchase of the Highland ideal at Balmoral, and her building of a 'new' castle there in 1848, was far more decisive. The new Balmoral – designed by William Smith with Prince Albert – comprised two blocks linked by a 80ft tower. Inside, the ballroom was ostentatiously decorated with stags' heads.

By the early 1840s, Bryce had been inspired by Billings' drawings to create a new dynamic Baronialism, far removed from the static two-dimensionality of Balmoral. The dramatic, cliff-top Seacliffe House (1841) was massive and turreted. Next, came the supreme Romanticism of Balfour Castle on the tiny island of Shapinsay, Orkney (1846–50), where a 'neat little villa' was swamped beneath a blanket of Baronial detailing, including Bryce's trademark: a thrusting bay window perched above a flat gable. Throughout his work, Bryce used standard elements of Baronial architecture, as illustrated by Billings. The most widely used of these motifs were: the Seton tower of Fyvie (Craigends, 1857–9), the round tower of Castle Fraser (Ballikinrain, from 1864), Castlemilk (from 1864) and the tower and oriel window combination of Maybole (Hartrigge, 1854 and the Glen, 1855–60).

Bryce also developed a new, Franco-Scotch Baronialism. Billings had claimed that Scottish Renaissance castles had been built by French masons, and this, according to his theory, explained why they recalled that country's 'airy turrets and fantastic tracery'. This claim was later rejected (along with many others by Billings) by MacGibbon and Ross in their *Castellated and Domestic Architecture of Scotland* (1887–92), which aimed to put the whole subject on an academic footing. The symmetrical tendencies of the Scottish Renaissance 'originals' were obviously a stimulus: already, in 1840–1, Bryce and Burn had embellished Thirlestane with yet further turrets and flanking wings. However the climax of the Franco-Scottish tendency was an Edinburgh school, Fettes College (1864–70). Bryce's own perspective presented the building asymmetrically, but the college's main, axial avenue to the south added yet another grand vista to Romantic Edinburgh [**colour plate 21**].

Edinburgh in this period saw a vigorous redevelopment drive, based on a City Improvement Act (passed 1867), as in Glasgow and Dundee. But in this case, the romantic principles already established by Thomas Hamilton and Burn now led to a Scotch Baronial street architecture. The linking of the tenement with the national was a crucial development. Billings had drawn attention to the 'peculiarities and merits' of old burghs and soon afterwards a Baronial improvement scheme was promoted privately in the city, by the 1853 Edinburgh Railway Station Access Act, to build a curving street from the High Street down to the new station. The Act specified that the new buildings must 'preserve as far as possible the architectural style' of the area. The resulting scheme, Cockburn Street (designed in c.1859–64 by Peddie & Kinnear) provided a new, romantic architectural gateway to the Old Town [**colour plate 23**].

Having taken on this new urban association, the Scotch Baronial style soon spread to other buildings. From the 1850s,

[75] **Aberdeen Town House (1866–74)**

Slightly later, Scotch Baronial began to spread to urban public buildings, beginning with the series of courthouses following the Sheriff Courthouses Act. Peddie & Kinnear's Greenock Sheriff Courthouse (1864–7), was a miniature Fettes-like composition with symmetrical central tower. From Baronial Sheriff courthouses to municipal buildings was a short step. An early pointer was Charles Wilson's Rutherglen (1862), followed by Bryce at Lockerbie (planned 1873, built from 1884). The greatest of these was undoubtedly the enlargement of Aberdeen Town House by Peddie & Kinnear. Its main tower, for several decades by far the most prominent

landmark in the city, echoed, in hugely amplified form, the old Schoolhill mansions of Aberdeen which had been illustrated by Billings.

the style began to be associated with projects for 'national monuments'. Bryce's pupil, J.T. Rochead, designed the earliest and grandest of these: the National Wallace Monument at Stirling (1859–69). The colossal, sculptural tower was 220 feet high, set on a prominent hill and constructed of rock-faced rubble, topped by the imperial emblem of a crown spire.

NEO-GOTHIC

During the first half of the nineteenth century, ecclesiastical buildings began to reflect the new emphasis on historical 'accuracy'. In contrast to England, France and Germany, where the Gothic was regarded as a 'national' style, Scotland lacked any emotional connection with Gothic. This allowed not only a thriving classical church architecture, but also the use of a wide range of other medieval styles, unconcerned with reaching a 'true' Gothic. The emphasis on achieving a 'national' neo-medievalism in church architecture would develop later. For the moment, most of the large numbers of Gothic churches built after 1800 were treated in a thin, spiky manner, with, if anything, English Perpendicular stylistic features which echoed a similar interest in English secular patterns during Scotland's 'North British' phase: for example, Glenorchy Church (1810–11), built by the Earl of Breadalbane as a kind of eye-catcher on rising ground; or Fetteresso Church, Stonehaven (1810–12). In Glasgow, celebrating the passing of the Catholic Relief Act, James Gillespie Graham designed St Andrew's R.C. Chapel (1814–17) with an imposing 'Oxbridge college chapel' front also seen in King's College, Aberdeen [6].

Of all the earlier axially-placed churches the greatest is one we have already encountered in our discussion of monumental Edinburgh: Gillespie Graham's Tolbooth Church on Edinburgh's Castlehill (1839–44). The 240ft-high steeple presents a cluster of soaring gablets, its mass lightened in a presentiment of the Glaswegian neo-Gothic of the 1860s and 1870s. In much of the detailing of the building (especially on the spire), Graham was helped by his young English assistant, A.W.N. Pugin – whose polemics were shortly to spark off the 'Gothic Revival' movement in his own country.

Throughout Europe, the interest in medieval architecture had now grown to the extent that objections arose over the condition of some of its monuments: the epoch of 'restoration' had begun. William Burn subjected Dunfermline to radical rebuilding in 1821, and in 1829–33 refaced St Giles' Cathedral Edinburgh, sweeping away the famous 'Luckenbooths' (medieval shops) attached to its walls. In 1836 Gillespie Graham produced plans for re-ordering Glasgow Cathedral internally. On the whole the national/moral passion, and later, indignation, provoked by church restoration in some countries (such as Germany or England) was less pronounced in Scotland. Conservationist energies instead were put into 'national' secular buildings such as castles, palaces and burghs. However, the focus on this material culture began much earlier, with Sir Walter Scott.

[76] **Abbotsford, Borders (1817–23)**
As part of his influence in creating the new 'image' of Scotland, it was Sir Walter Scott who played a decisive role in setting down precise 'national' qualities in architecture. Scott's writings played a key role in the international development of Romanticism, by identifying romantic genius with nations. The influence Scott exerted on the development of 'national romanticism' in architecture was not, however, purely literary. He also made a crucial impact through the building of his own famous romantic retreat in the Borders: Abbotsford.

The building of Abbotsford took place in two stages from 1817–23, after several attempts at design by Scott himself, attempting to give shape to his abstract antiquarian notions. Scott's first architect-collaborator on the Abbotsford project was William Stark, who began work in 1811 on what was envisaged as a 'whimsical, gay, odd cabin', but soon became 'an old English hall'. By 1816, the 'English' features had gone in favour of a specifically 'Scottish' image: an old-fashioned Scotch residence'. In the second phase,

built 1821–3, Scott's ideas took the shape of some explicitly 'Baronial' features – including a Fyvie-type arch flanked by crow-stepped towers on the river façade. [colour plate 22]

Inside, Scott wanted an 'old' look which he achieved through the displaying of historical 'fragments' and by the use of distressed decoration 'in strict imitation of oak or cedar'. The interior was to appear 'as if it had stood untouched for years'.

The influence of Abbotsford was enormous – and not only within architecture. Where Scott's works had promoted Scotland as an international tourist attraction, Abbotsford now itself became part of that tourist circuit. In 1844, Fox Talbot photographed the house for a book, Sun Pictures in Scotland – only the second photographic book ever published – devoted to subjects associated with Scott and his novels. By the mid-1850s, Abbotsford was receiving over 4000 visitors a year, and by the mid-1870s over 2000 Americans alone were visiting annually. (Visitors are brought in via the servants' entrance, as seen in the photograph opposite.)

[77] St Mary's Cathedral, Edinburgh (1874–1917)

Large Episcopal commissions included G.F. Bodley's sumptuously ornamented city mission church at St Salvador's Dundee (1865–75), and a series of churches or cathedrals by Gilbert Scott, beginning with St Paul's Dundee (1852), St Mary's Glasgow (from 1871), and culminating in Scott's victory in the 1872 competition for St Mary's Cathedral in Edinburgh. St Mary's was begun in 1874 as a centralised design in heavy rubble masonry with single spire, but two western spires were added later (and completed 1917), creating the fantastic, Schinkel-like vista we enjoy today along neo-classical Melville Street. In keeping with Tractarian emphasis on 'local' features, these designs by Scott or Butterfield attempted to incorpo-

rate 'Scottish' medieval details, in the same way that Scott's Nikolaikirche had clothed its powerful spire in 'German' forms.

[78] Glasgow University (1864–70)

Within the broad framework of eclecticism, neo-Gothic was, of course, regarded as appropriate for churches.

What about non-ecclesiastical buildings? Throughout the 19th century this was generally regarded as inappropriate, but there was a brief fashion for such buildings in the 1860s and 1870s. This was seemingly sparked off by the work of Scott at the Albert Institute, Dundee (1864–7), and the new Glasgow University building (1864–70, with spire 1887 by J.O. Scott). At Glasgow, Scott's engagement proved controversial, as did the Gothic style, which Alexander Thomson decried as an 'invasion from the south'. Nevertheless, Scott's design followed the Gothic Revivalist formula of seeking legitimacy through 'Scottish' decoration. The photograph shows the University quadrangles before the construction of the Bute and Randolph Halls, completed by Scott's son, J. Oldrid Scott, along with the spire. J. J. Burnet's War Memorial Chapel of 1923–7 later enclosed the west quadrangle.

[79] **British Linen Bank, St Andrew Square, Edinburgh (1846–51)**

The palazzo theme of bank architecture was developed by David Bryce in central Edinburgh over thirty years: the Refuge Assurance Building (1840); the Edinburgh Life Assurance Company offices in George Street (1843) and the Union Bank Edinburgh office in George Street (1874). The simple style was adaptable to modern needs but the demand for richness grew with Edinburgh's

continued development as an important financial centre. David Rhind's 1843 design for the Commercial Bank included 'gorgeous' interior plasterwork, but David Bryce's British Linen Bank, on the east side of St Andrew Square, took expensive classical complexity to a climax. Here, six tall Corinthian columns, ostentatiously set forward on a massive ground-floor podium, support statues by A. Handyside Ritchie; inside, the columned telling

hall continues the monumental theme. Bryce's later rebuilding (1864–70) of the Bank of Scotland head office at the top of the Mound gave the architect a site which lay at the very centre of Edinburgh's scenic amphitheatre, a potent symbol of the new wealth. The main north front was set on a colossal basement and broke out into a Corinthian-columned, pedimented centrepiece, flanked by towers and crowned by a thrusting dome.

James Gowans (1821–90)

James Gowans was an idiosyncratic follower of the 'harmonic' principles of rationalist architecture developed in opposition to the flashy brilliance of Bryce's bank architecture. Gowans was an architect/contractor for the Highland Railway and the Edinburgh tramway system, and built up one of the biggest quarrymaster's business in Scotland. Understandably, he became an upholder of the capital's status as a stone-built city, and participated in the regulation of building activity, becoming Lord Dean of Guild in 1885. At the same time, Gowans championed the cause of 'sanitary' working-class dwellings. Taking up the conception that 'in architecture, a geometric basis is at the root of what we admire', Gowans applied it to masonry construction, believing that he had discovered the key to medieval masonry design. And he was able to build realisations of his ideas. His Edinburgh house, 'Rockville' (1858), was a stone grid of two-foot squares of rubble – supposedly designed to allow mass production of stone components. With Gowans' work, and that of his sometime collaborator, F.T. Pilkington, we see rationalism cracking under the strain of a romantic tendency to perceive a kind of mystical reality in the apparently ordinary business of stone construction. This was by no means an eccentric Scottish concern, but part of an attempt to 'see' beyond the outward appearance of things to an underlying truth. Geometry provided the ideal basis for this new stone mysticism.

[81] **James Gowans: 'Rockville', Edinburgh (1858)**

Scott's fame was the inspiration for the most spectacular shrine of the early nineteenth century: the Sir Walter Scott Monument in Edinburgh. This 200ft-high neo-Gothic steeple with its flying-buttressed base (statue by John Steell) was designed by George Meikle Kemp and built in 1840–6 [**colour plate 24**]. The completed monument was hailed by a Town Council brochure as a 'Gothic temple … gorgeously decorated … perhaps the finest monumental edifice in the kingdom'. Kemp predicted that the views from it would 'create an excitement something like one of Scott's romances', recalling Scott's own presentation of Edinburgh during the royal visit in 1822, but also presaging Geddes's idea of 'outlook' stimulating community.

As far as specifically Scottish Gothic churches were concerned – churches that resembled historic prototypes – the idea was generally undermined until late in the century by a belief that, in Alexander Thomson's words, the Gothic was 'not national'. The Gothic remained a 'style' rather than a moral crusade, as it was in England. If anything, Scotland's answer to Pugin's determination to revive the true Christian architecture was the spiritual classicism of Thomson.

During the 1850s, Presbyterian neo-Gothic continued the Gillespie Graham formula of church and axial steeple, perhaps with more 'correct' detailing. By the 1860s, however, some Free Church congregations had confidence enough to look for new patterns. The most important of these were designed by Frederick T. Pilkington, who built (in partnership with John F. Bell) an eclectic series of churches, beginning with Trinity Free Church, Irvine, and Barclay Church, Edinburgh, both in 1861. Trinity mingled French and Italian Gothic, but Barclay Church was even more ambitious. At 250 feet, its vigorously modelled steeple was the tallest in Scotland.

The 1860s and 1870s saw the first comprehensive attempts to evoke the spirit of Scottish medieval architecture in line with the castle revival. Bryce's Carnwath (1865–9) referred to the nearby ruined collegiate chapel in the same contextual way that his Broadstone House (1869) at Port Glasgow would recall the seventeenth-century Newark Castle, directly below the site. J.T. Rochead's Park Church (1856–7) had gabletted windows on the side façades, a feature inspired by Elgin Cathedral and St Giles. A similar arrangement exists at Dowanhill Church (U.P.,1865–6) by William Leiper.

Dowanhill's massive preaching space was fronted by a Normandy Gothic steeple. Inside, the galleries face a tabernacled pulpit set high in the far wall, reached by a concealed entrance as in Thomson's slightly earlier St Vincent Street Church, also for the United Presbyterians. Although, in general, there seemed little affinity between Leiper's soaring design and Thomson's architecture of mass, there was in fact a direct link: a decorative scheme by Daniel Cottier, whose designs, at Dowanhill as at the contemporary Queen's Park, signalled the beginnings of the rejection of mid-nineteenth-century eclecticism as garish. Cottier provided a scheme of stencil work in tertiary colours, defined in black and gold, stained glass (with foliage and Old Testament figurative subjects), and ceiling decoration which comprised a vast painted sky of stars and planets.

THE SITUATION IN 1880

Around 1880, a pent-up dam of classical restraint in architecture seemed finally to burst. There followed a torrent of 'free' (or Northern Renaissance) architecture, specialising in richly encrusted buildings which heaped detail upon tiny detail. In this movement, Rowand Anderson at first led the way. In 1882–4, in the most important Glasgow commercial development of the decade – the Caledonian Railway headquarters block at Central Station (completed as a hotel) [82] – Anderson balanced a busily gabled façade with a massive vertical punctuation in the sheer, tall corner tower, crowned by gables. A similar theme of elaboration punctuated by bold verticality was

[82] Rowand Anderson: Central Station Hotel, Glasgow (1882–4), extended by James Miller (1900–8)

achieved slightly later at Glasgow City Chambers, but there the style was florid Italian Renaissance and the tower, neo-Thomson.

As an essentially 'applied' style – as in the sixteenth- and seventeenth-century castles of the north-east of Scotland – the Northern Renaissance allowed the big new office blocks to be articulated with decoration. The most important exponent was A.G. Sydney Mitchell, who used his Northern Renaissance 'house style' for a series of banks and commercial buildings, including large numbers of Commercial Bank branches built from 1883. Sydney Mitchell was also involved in loosening the classical strictures of Edinburgh private dwellings and, later, had a hand in designing Glasgow's only 'free' terrace composition at Great Western Road in 1904–6 at Lowther Terrace [83].

[83] James Miller: No.8 (1904) and No.10 (*c*.1900) Lowther Terrace; A.G. Sydney Mitchell: No.9 Lowther Terrace (1904–6) – Glasgow

[84] Cluny Castle, Aberdeenshire (late 16th c.)

The publication between 1887–92 of the five-volume set of David MacGibbon and Thomas Ross's The Castellated and Domestic Architecture of Scotland was of immense importance to the study and appreciation of Scottish architecture. The move towards a more 'archaeological' rather than picturesque approach to the subject was gradually being made but their massive effort gathered up all the individual pieces of antiquarian knowledge and presented it critically – often very critically. Their main target was Billings. Perhaps with some irony, they wrote that 'Our sketches are not intended to imitate or rival the beautiful and artistic etchings of some of our Scottish edifices which have, from time to time been published.' Instead they wished to record, to measure, and to classify according to plan type. Even where no building existed, as at Cluny (above), they succeeded in obtaining the drawings of others, fully acknowledged. In this case the drawings and descriptions were made by James Skene of Rubislaw (1775–1864), antiquarian and friend of Walter Scott.

[85] James Thomson: Connal Building, West George Street, Glasgow (1898–1900)

In some higher-rent tenement blocks, the tenement issue was spectacularly dealt with, as in Burnet's Charing Cross Mansions (1891). This design's staggering grandeur made a crucial differentiation between the 'ordinary' tenement and high class 'flatted town houses'.

Towards the end of the century, Northern Renaissance became, almost exclusively, the language of commercialism, confined to the production of bulky commercial buildings, such as Jenners store (1893–5) or the North British Hotel (1896–1902) in Edinburgh or the vast red sandstone chambers of Glasgow such as James Thomson's Connal building [85]. Soon, the idea that 'national' characteristics could be evoked simply by apply-

ing detail began to seem trite. In Glasgow, James Salmon brought a refreshing simplicity to the problem at Mercantile Chambers (1897–8) which The Builder thought 'excessively plain' but 'daringly original' in its use of attenuated Art Nouveau detailing. In Edinburgh – quite typically – it was the architect involved in introducing a movement who led its overthrow. In 1897 Rowand Anderson completed his Edinburgh University extension scheme, the McEwan Hall, which returned to a more stately interpretation of the Renaissance. These were attempts at organising the chaos of architectural production, but soon the whole business of architecture as an art would be put under review by its leading exponents.

[86]   **Forth Bridge under construction (1882–90) (contemporary photograph)**

Along with their conventional eclectic output of stations, hotels and offices, the later 19th-century railway companies built daring structures, such as the double-cantilever Forth Bridge (Sir John Fowler and Sir Benjamin Baker). For the railways' conventional buildings, James Miller monopolised the work. The most prolific railway architect in the pre-war years, he designed everything from station frontages to tenements, office blocks and hotels.

In the period up to the First World War, Scotland became one of the richest countries in the world. That wealth brought a confidence which was ostentatiously expressed through architecture. But during this period of cataclysmic change, architecture was also to undergo its final, fundamental transformation. What had been a royal art, a noble art and, eventually, a civic art, was set to become a social art.

The years from around 1880 in Scotland, as elsewhere in Europe, saw a rejection of mass-produced ornament. After the busy intensity of late nineteenth-century commercial architecture, an appeal for calm went out. To 'advanced' architects, the complex eclecticism of buildings like the North British Hotel now seemed tasteless. The solution to the problem took apparently opposing forms: one that looked across the Atlantic, and another that looked in on Scotland – back, once again, to the so-called 'traditional' Scottish architecture of the seventeenth century. The leader of the Traditionalist tendency was Rowand Anderson, and it was later taken forward by Robert Lorimer. However, in architecture as elsewhere, nothing is ever that simple, for the supreme exponent of Anderson and Lorimer's Traditionalism came not from the patrician world of establishment Edinburgh, but from the great industrial city of Glasgow. His name was Charles Rennie Mackintosh. First, we must go back to the source of Traditionalism.

ROWAND ANDERSON AND TRADITIONALISM

There had been attempts at architectural reforms typical of the palace revolutions in art which demand plainness after excess, but Traditionalism went much deeper, striking at the heart of commercial society itself. Now, the world of architecture was seen as money-grabbing and coarse, part of a vulgar 'industry'. The task of reinvesting architecture with a moral purpose was informed by research into a pre-industrial golden age. The new focus of this concern was the 'home': the 'ordinary' dwellings of middle-class or working-class people.

The focus on the 'home' was defined in Scotland to embrace not only the middle-class villa, but also the housing and 'community' of the 'traditional' burgh. However, the initial efforts of Anderson and others were concerned with the bourgeois house, where they rapidly became bound up with the new 'artistic' tendencies in the work of designers such as Cottier and J.J. Stevenson.

Anderson's most influential domestic project was his own villa in Colinton, 'Allermuir' (1879). Its basic shape came from Baronial houses like Bryce's Shambellie (1856) and seventeenth-century houses like Pinkie, but Anderson was no admirer of Bryce's towers and turrets, or his plate glass and machine-cut stone. At Allermuir, he wanted to create more than just an image [87]. His vision was of a deeper, textured oldness shorn of flashy rhetoric. Internally, the 'comfort' of the 'artistic' house resulted not only from the avoidance of bright

[87] Rowand Anderson: 'Allermuir', Colinton, Edinburgh (1879)

[88] Scotland Street School, Glasgow (1902–6)

Provision of schools increased hugely after the passing of the 1878 Education Act. Edinburgh school architecture, overseen by Robert Wilson and later J.A. Carfrae, developed along classical lines, consistent with the 'academy' ideal. Glasgow and the surrounding burghs employed many architects, including C.R. Mackintosh. The varied architectural solutions for hospitals continued: from high-density patterns (e.g. T.G. Abercrombie's Royal Alexandra Infirmary, Paisley (1896–1900), or James Miller's Glasgow Royal Infirmary rebuilding (1907–14) following a 1901 competition) to pavilion plans for infectious diseases hospitals such as Thomson & Sandilands', Stobhill (1904).

daylighting, and from the artfully plain internal timber details, but also from its Abbotsford-like bricolage of antiques and plate.

By the turn of the century, the most successful exponent of the 'cult of the house' in the East was Robert S. Lorimer. Lorimer applied the approach not only to new projects, in a series of plain, harled villas, beginning with gabled The Grange, North Berwick (1893), but also in restorations of old houses, from Earlshall in 1890–4 to Balmanno in 1916. The Glasgow commercial work of architects such as Burnet and Campbell, in its open embrace of modernity, was anathema to Lorimer.

Later, Lorimer took the textured rubble of Traditionalist architecture to an astonishing extreme. At Rowallan (1902) and

Ardkinglas (1905–7), he developed a 'Scotch style' consisting in bare rubble walls with archaic classicising detail. The tension between rhetoric and restraint was almost broken at Formakin (1912–14), built for the stockbroker John A. Holms. This was an austere, almost primitive exterior, with punched-in apertures and thick-jointed rubble whose internal climax was a first-floor great chamber of massive size.

From the 1890s, this relatively exuberant Scots Renaissance style was extended to other secular building types such as Burnet and Campbell's Glasgow Western Infirmary Pathology Building (1894), and T.G. Abercrombie's Paisley Royal Alexandra Infirmary (1896–1900), built in the form of a keep with wings. Rubble massiveness also spread, during the 1880s and

[89] City Chambers, Glasgow (1883–8)

In 1900, Glasgow was at its 'world city' peak, but there were already signs of distress. Confidence in Glasgow as a force for good was badly shaken by reports of hunger and disease. The paternalism of the city fathers was now challenged by working-class politics, which increasingly focused on housing conditions. However, the cities and large burghs were still seen as centres of 'improvement'. Glasgow led the way in this epoch of 'municipal socialism', introducing a huge range of services from water supply to street

lighting. Like the British Empire, Glasgow surged forwards and outwards. The city's progress was symbolised in its new municipal buildings, built to the designs of William Young. Local, national and British symbolism was employed at the 1883 foundation ceremony and in the completed building. The entrance façade featured a 'Jubilee' pediment depicting Queen Victoria receiving homage from the empire. Glasgow's improving example was echoed in grand classical projects for municipal buildings throughout the Central Belt.

[90] 'Fine Arts', Glasgow Exhibition (1911)

The search for the 'national' was now taken up, even in the internationalist city of Glasgow. The building type which highlighted the redefinition of the nation was the national or international exhibition. There were five such events before 1914: two in Edinburgh (1886, 1908) and three in Glasgow (1888, 1901 and 1911). At first the appropriate architecture style was seen as exotic, but in 1911 the entire Glasgow exhibition was in a sober Scottish Renaissance style. This was the start of the idea of the exhibitions as an ideological rather than a purely commercial

showcase for the nation. At the Scottish Exhibition of National History, Art and Industry, in Glasgow, history displaced industry: the architectural style adopted was Stewart palace Baronial, along with an almost proto-Disney 'Auld Toun', and a realistic thatched-house settlement. The years after 1910 also saw the 'restoration' of particularly spectacularly-sited castles in rock-faced rubble. The most ambitious was Major John MacRae-Gilstrap's costly conversion of Eilean Donan Castle (from 1913–32) from a ruin to a huge, block-like complex, in rubble inside and out, designed by Edinburgh architect George Mackie Watson.

1890s, to municipal buildings. Anderson inflated his plain, crow-stepped classical style into this more imposing mode at Pollokshaws Burgh Buildings (1895–8).

Along with the chauvinistic strain in Scottish Traditionalism, there came a belief in the use of Baronialism to reform working-class housing along 'artistic', burgh-community lines. The focus of this tendency during the period up to the First World War was the 'Old Edinburgh' movement: an admiration of the dilapidated Old Town. Where Scott's influence had fired the imagination of Baronial country-house builders, now the city had Robert Louis Stevenson's 'very metropolis of squalor, yet likewise of Romance'. But it was one thing to con-

ceptualise the Old Town as a romantic cluster, why not build in its image? Sydney Mitchell's Well Court, Edinburgh – a complex of working-class tenements commissioned by *Scotsman* publisher J.R. Findlay – attempted to do just that. Well Court was a kind of sanitised 'slum': a dense block, with communal facilities, arranged around a garden courtyard, with picturesque grouping, steep roofs and small windows.

Well Court's Old Town image stimulated the imagination of one of Scotland's most remarkable thinkers, Patrick Geddes [91]. In 1883, for reasons of patriotism and civic pride, Geddes decided to try to revive the eighteenth-century 'Golden Age' of Edinburgh University and Old Town. As a biologist, Geddes saw the Old Town as a diseased organism which could be 're-generated'. He began to buy decayed tenements and undeveloped sites, and started a programme of 'conservative surgery', designed to revitalise the Old Town as a 'university city'. The reconditioned blocks were ornamented with picturesque timber outshots, and interspersed with 'reclaimed' garden spaces. Geddes' most spectacular building achievement was Ramsay Garden, a development overlooking the city; a coloured, turret-encrusted fantasy [**colour plate 26**]. In spite of these efforts, Geddes became convinced that the main thrust of sanitary working-class housebuilding must be in the form of garden city cottages. Rosyth, built from 1914, and a Clydeside equivalent at Westerton (1913–15), would serve as training-grounds for a generation of Scots garden suburb architects, such as A.H. Mottram and J.A.W. Grant.

CHURCHES

Within Presbyterian architecture, the loss of the churches' social role in favour, mainly, of the municipalities, was offset by a new emphasis on 'worship' for its own sake. This essentially neo-Catholic liturgical movement was part of an international Protestant tendency. Within Roman Catholicism, there was a complementary trend which produced large, hall-like churches with ancillary suites of buildings like their Protestant counterparts.

How could Presbyterian churches be made more 'worshipful'? The decisive steps had been taken in the 1880s by Rowand Anderson in a cathedral-like layout at the new Govan Parish

[**91**] **Patrick Geddes (1865–1932)**

In the character of a medieval scholar (c.1912–13).

Church (designed 1882, built 1884–8). The theme was then taken up by Burnet at Barony Church (1886–90) and on a smaller scale at a series of squat, primitivist churches such as St Molio's, Arran (1886) [92], and culminating in the Gardner Memorial Church, Brechin (1896–1900). The most lavish projects of the age were commissioned by magnates: for example, Coats Memorial Church (Paisley), with its marbled sanctuary-baptistry and crown steeple, or Clark Memorial Church, Largs (1892, by T.G. Abercrombie). Sydney Mitchell secured several large commissions, including the Memorial Church at Crichton Royal Hospital (1888–97), and Belford Church, Edinburgh (1888), while Leiper built his St Columba, Kilmacolm (1901–3), a massive 'Franco-Scottish' creation.

The most emphatic example of the nationalist trend in church architecture expressed an extreme form of imperial Scottish patriotism: Lorimer's Thistle Chapel, built in 1909–11 to affirm Scottish aristocratic loyalty to the British crown [93]. The tall chapel had a Roslin-like elaboration, carried out by Edinburgh craft designers. This can be contrasted with Burnet's simpler evocation of archaic monumentality which avoided the expense of a soaring tower.

At two monumental but small churches of 1911 by Ramsay Traquair (Christian Scientist Church, Edinburgh) and Reginald Fairlie (Our Lady of the Assumption, Troon), the fifteenth-century Scots neo-Romanesque tradition was evoked. By that time, a more general revival of Scottish ecclesiastical forms was well underway. Crown steeples had been increasingly popular since the mid 1880s: they were particularly favoured by J.J. Stevenson (St Leonard's, Perth, 1885; Nathaniel Stevenson Memorial Free Church, Glasgow, 1898–1902; and Peter Memorial Church, Stirling, 1901).

Within church design of the 1930s a classic Traditionalist tendency emerged. The most striking realisations were in the Roman Catholic Church, where since the pontificate of Pius X (1903–14) a movement towards centralised, worshipper-centred plans had been growing. This would culminate in the 1960s, in the work of Pope John XXIII and the Second Vatican Council, but already by the 1930s a move towards basilican plans was underway across northern Europe.

The key innovator was Giacomo Antonio (Jack) Coia. Taught at Glasgow School of Art, Coia had trained in a number of Glasgow offices, and the deaths of Gillespie and William Kidd had left him sole heir to their practice. Coia's first church, St Anne's, Dennistoun (1931), exploited engineering skills in

[92] J.J. Burnet: St Molio's Church, Arran (1886)

[93] Robert Lorimer: Thistle Chapel, annexe to St Giles', Edinburgh (1909–11)

[94] John Patrick, 3rd Marquess of Bute (1847–1902)

As with initiatives as diverse as parks, libraries and art galleries, the aristocracy at first took the lead in conservation. John Kinross's restoration of the chapel range and gatehouse at Falkland (1887) was only one of a string of projects by the 3rd Marquess of Bute, in this case backed up by research into the Lord Treasurer's and Master of Works' Accounts. State intervention in preservation had begun with the 1882 Ancient Monuments Act, and, following pressure by the Edinburgh Professor Gerard Baldwin Brown, the Royal Commission on Ancient Monuments was founded in 1908 and a second Ancient Monuments Act was passed in 1913.

[95] Scottish National Portrait Gallery, Edinburgh (1884–9)

Rowand Anderson brought the block theme to maturity at the Scottish National Portrait Gallery and National Museum, the climax of a long campaign for the building of a national pantheon. The design repeated the block shape of Mount Stuart, but added corner spires and contrasted the ornate central entrance bay with a vast expanse of bare upper walling. Evoking as it did the Doge's Palace, Anderson's Portrait Gallery's style was whimsically taken up and elaborated by Leiper in the spectacular Venetian façade of the Templeton Carpet Factory, Glasgow (1889).

[96] Marischal College, Aberdeen (1893–8)

The most significant use of medieval styles outwith churches was one of

Scotland's greatest 19th-century secular works: A. Marshall Mackenzie's Perpendicular style extension to Marischal College, whose soaring tower departed radically from Simpson's earlier collegiate horizontality, and paralleled the American trend towards 'skyscraper Perpendicular' for such buildings.

true Beaux-Arts fashion, to obtain a broad centralised space flanked by narrow arcades rather than aisles. Its monumental façade was red-brick and classical with Byzantine elements. Coia's larger churches of the 1940s and early 1950s often featured triangular 'Gothic' elements. The largest and most powerful was St Lawrence, Greenock (1951–4), a stepped group sited on a huge substructure, with a dramatically lit interior.

The Church of Scotland's 1950s buildings were much simpler and homelier evocations of Traditionalism, inspired by the examples of Alan Reiach and Robert Hurd's *Building Scotland* (1941) [117]. Kininmonth's Drylaw (1955–6) was a geometrical, rendered group with swept-down pitched roofs, and Ian G. Lindsay & Partners' Livingston Station and Colinton Mains (1949 and 1954) even more closely evoked the pyramidal-towered, eighteenth-century Caithness parish churches, such as Reay, illustrated in Reiach and Hurd's book.

CHARLES RENNIE MACKINTOSH

One of the key elements in the architectural reaction to the chaos of late nineteenth-century commercial architecture was a retreat into artistic individualism. This tendency took its most extravagant form in the 'Glasgow Style' pioneered by 'The Four': the designers Margaret and Frances Macdonald, and the two architects they later married, Charles Rennie Mackintosh and Herbert MacNair. The Glasgow Style developed one aspect of the 'artistic house' in particular: the ideal of the totally designed interior. Like Robert Adam and Alexander Thomson, Mackintosh employed architecture as an all-embracing art.

In common with Lorimer, Mackintosh insisted on composed space, in opposition to 'clutter'. Mackintosh departed from mainstream Traditionalism, however, in his emotional intensity. In contrast to Lorimer, whose spacious rooms, dotted with antiques and tapestries, seemed haphazard, Mackintosh began by creating a neutral background in which darkness and light were contrasted. Against this background were set very limited areas of decoration, such as symbolist gesso panels by Macdonald. Then came the furniture, made and placed by the artists themselves.

Charles Rennie Mackintosh (1868–1928)

Charles Rennie Mackintosh was one of eleven children of William McIntosh, a Glasgow policeman of Irish descent, and Margaret Rennie from Ayr. His abilities were noticed when he enrolled as a sixteen-year-old part-time student at Glasgow School of Art, during his apprenticeship with John Hutchison. In 1890, Mackintosh won the Alexander Thomson travelling scholarship and went to France and Italy. He made his mark with the firm of Honeyman and Keppie, which he joined as a draughtsman in 1889 and became a partner in 1901. The pinnacle of Mackintosh's career was the delayed design of Glasgow Art School's western end, including the library interior. In 1913, after a series of disappointments, Mackintosh left Glasgow for good. He devoted much of the rest of his life to painting and textile design, although there were smaller, but significant architectural projects such as the re-modelling of Derngate, Northamptonshire in 1913. Mackintosh died in London at the age of sixty.

[97]
F.H. Newbery:
'Charles Rennie
Mackintosh'
(1914)

rooms. In the dining-room design, a pale ceiling and floor contrasted with the gravity of vertically gridded, dark-stained wall-panels, inset with decorative rectangles. In the similarly proportioned music-room, a light grey background, with sparing, asymmetrically-placed furniture was offset by splashes of red and blue, by large symbolist panels, and by an ornate piano with baldacchino.

[100 & 101] Glasgow School of Art (1905–9)

Mackintosh's final built masterpiece was the west wing of the Glasgow School of Art (below). Like the contem-

porary work of Campbell or Joass (who trained in Glasgow under Burnet), the exterior modelling was dominated by linear verticality. Its gabled west façade featured tall, flat-topped oriel projections fronting the library; the south façade contrasted with this, its complex pattern of recessed windows and voids, with small calculated elements of irregularity, recalling the sculptural decoration around James IV's east façade gateway at Linlithgow. Internally, the library – perhaps Mackintosh's most renowned interior (opposite) – exploited the Glasgow shipfitting skills of prefabricated timber assembly to create a complex decorated grid of galleries and supports.

[98] Interior of Hill House, Helensburgh (1902–4)

The crucial series of domestic interiors began in 1899–1900: the remodelling of the Dunglass Castle drawing-room, and of Mackintosh and Macdonald's house at 120 Mains Street, Glasgow (now Blythswood Street); and the building of Windyhill, Kilmacolm. Then, in 1902–4, came Hill House, Helensburgh, for the publisher Walter Blackie. At Hill House, Mackintosh placed a highly individual dwelling into the rationalist suburban grid of a

seaside commuter town on the Firth of Clyde, which from its conformist roots had already grown into an architecturally chaotic suburb by the end of the 19th century.

[99] House for an Art Lover, Glasgow (1901)

The climax of the Mackintoshes' interior work was their entry in a 1901 competition for a 'House for an Art Lover'. Here Mackintosh exaggerated the traditional division between dark 'masculine' and light 'feminine'

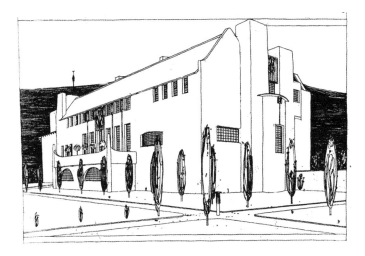

From the outside, the white-harled Hill House was reticent to the point of being grim. Mackintosh managed to achieve a whiteness through the use – for the first time – of Portland cement in the render. Externally, there were only a few hints of the lightness of the interior, such as the jutting, square bay window, which pointed to a Modernist breaking down of the external and internal divide. Generally, in Mackintosh's external architecture, the stress was close in spirit to Lorimer's 'national' architecture. Even the stylistically advanced west wing of the School of Art referred to James IV's gateway at Linlithgow. The only true model, in Mackintosh's view, was Scotland's historical architecture, and at Hill House he employed a familiar hall-and-tower typology, with a lower domestic block answered by a tight L-plan group, complete with service stair in the re-entrant angle. The understated entrance to the house is on the west flank, where the composition conforms most closely to the contemporary English Arts and Crafts work of Voysey and others.

Inside, all the main rooms face south, including the library and business-room located, as was traditional, close to the entrance. Next was the drawing-room, which was at the very heart of the house in all its deeply 'feminine', passive splendour. The billiard-room and den had been dropped from the plans at Walter Blackie's insistence, leaving the tiny library and smaller dining-room as the only traditionally 'male' spaces. The cult of the house had been driven by a desire to create a haven of femininity, but this also underscored the idea of the house as a 'woman's place'. The service wing was on the east flank, with a day nursery, children's bedrooms and schoolroom above. A traditional Scottish stair turret gave easy access to all floors for the servants. The pristine serenity of the house required constant maintenance. Economies were made in the garden of Hill House, which had been designed on Lorimerian formal lines, but this work was never carried out. A harled and slated gardener's store is composed with the main block in the manner of outwork remains such as Billings had illustrated at Newark (see also Craigievar, [23]).

Mackintosh also produced a series of tea-room interiors for Kate Cranston. At Buchanan Street (1896) and Argyle Street (1897), Mackintosh contributed, respectively, murals and furniture to an overall scheme by George Walton. At Ingram Street (1901) he and Macdonald took charge of the whole commission, which included a staircase and white dining-room. And at the Willow Tea Rooms (1903) their interiors included a flowing sequence of dark and light spaces on the ground floor, and culminated in the Room de Luxe, its focal point a gesso panel by Macdonald.

Apart from the Maclaren-influenced corner tower of the Glasgow Herald building (1893–4), the beginning of the mature phase of Mackintosh's architecture began in 1896 with the Glasgow School of Art. The design, built in two stages (completed 1909), was for a steeply sloping site like Maclaren's Stirling High School. The building is an 'E' plan, with asymmetrical north-facing main façade and three wings falling to the rear, in a composition which seems to recall the main front of Fyvie, but with Linlithgow-like elements and a tendency to Athenaeum-inspired verticality in the first phase to the east flank. Other turn-of-century commissions were treated with an austerity which offered originality on a budget: the soaring, bay-windowed Daily Record building (1900), a newspaper office crammed into a narrow lane in the centre of Glasgow, and Scotland Street School (1902) [88], its twin stairtowers combining an evocation of the Earl's Palace, Kirkwall, with bold fenestration.

Lorimer and Mackintosh are often characterised as opposite tendencies, but in fact Lorimer parallelled Mackintosh's 'cult of the white drawing-room', at Rowallan (from 1902), at Hyndford, North Berwick (1903), and in the remodelling of Dunrobin (from 1915). But in contrast to Mackintosh's intensity, Lorimer simply extended the scope of 'antique' collecting and furnishing into the eighteenth century, making backgrounds rather lighter. At Balmanno, for instance, he designed a floor plan for Whytock and Reid to supply imitation antiques. Lorimer's work was essentially part of a Europewide 'return' to classicism. This tendency soon spread to Traditionalist exteriors. From the 1900s, there was increasing symmetry, and a reassertion of 'Renaissance' horizontality of proportion. In his remodelling of Wemyss Hall (from 1905), Lorimer provided a symmetrical front with low overlooking formal terracing.

ECOLE DES BEAUX ARTS AND THOMSON'S LEGACY

In the 1880s, Scotland's devotion to monumental architecture and city planning was potentially compromised by a new stress on the use of individual buildings, rather than their appearance and relation to other buildings. In Glasgow, at the cutting edge of technology, there were urgent attempts to deal with this problem by marrying the functional and the stylistic. This was achieved through a renewed connection with France: this time through the rationalism of the Ecole des Beaux Arts in Paris, but also through a revival of the towering genius of Alexander Thomson.

The teaching of the Ecole des Beaux Arts combined an emphasis on function and plan with an external grandeur that was well suited to the Scottish monumental tradition. The Beaux-Arts tendency was international but, like all such movements, it varied significantly from country to country. The key figure in making the connection between the new – the Beaux Arts – and the old Thomson – was James Sellars. Sellars encouraged pupils to attend the Ecole, but his own buildings, such as St Andrew's Halls (1873–7) [102], triumphantly recalled Thomson's achievements. Beaux-Arts ideas entered Glasgow School of Art (from 1887) and the Glasgow and West of Scotland Technical College (from 1892). In 1904, after a deputation to Paris led by J.J. Burnet and W. Forrest Salmon, Eugène Bourdon was nominated to report on the reform of architectural education in Glasgow, and, following a merger of departments, was appointed first Professor of Architecture at the School of Art. The eventual leader of this new monumental tendency was the Glaswegian, Paris-trained architect, J.J. Burnet. On coming home to Glasgow, Burnet at first developed an austere French classicism, in lavish projects such as the Royal Glasgow Fine Art Institute of 1878–9, in which he blended 'refined Greek' with 'the full flowing lines of the Renaissance'. However, in 1886, he was joined in partnership by another Atelier Pascal pupil, J.A. Campbell, and the first of the new partnership's successive breakthroughs was made. In a dramatic elaboration of what was to come, at the Athenaeum Theatre (1891) in Glasgow [103], Burnet and Campbell vertically stacked a theatre, lunch rooms, offices, and a double height gymnasium onto a single house plot.

This new dynamism crucially influenced a completely new building type: the multi-storey office block. Here we see the growing fascination with America, as the United States emerged as the new symbol of modernity. Rising property values in central Glasgow prompted more intense land use and

[102] Mitchell Theatre, Glasgow (1873–7)

The Glasgow grid was firm but flexible in its mixture of uses, housed in eclectic, monumental buildings. Here James Sellars' St Andrew's Halls (now the Mitchell Theatre) on Granville Street is juxtaposed in sharp perspective with another of the architect's designs, Wylie & Lochhead's Cabinet Works, 1879.

there followed a rapid spread of tall office blocks, at first keeping to an older formula of heavy decoration. Soon, under the influence of the Athenaeum Theatre, there were attempts at bolder, 'modern' designs. Burnet's most striking skyscrapers, such as Atlantic Chambers (1899–1900) [104] and Waterloo Chambers (1898–1900), were designed after a visit to America in 1896, and by the turn of the century, the new multi-storey office style was being widely imitated. One of the most radically different was the glass wall of James Salmon's ten-storey St Vincent Chambers (1899).

Around 1907–12, regular steel frames were introduced in Scotland. This made asymmetrical or heavy façades relatively expensive, and so the Beaux Arts commercial style became more austere. A key turning point was Campbell pupil A.D. Hislop's Phoenix Assurance building, Glasgow (1912–13), with its granite, Doric-columned base and plain, flat upper storeys. Steel frames were later partially exposed through the use of bays articulated with bronze or copper.

In Edinburgh, 'traditional' classicism and Renaissance proportions had remained fairly constant but here, too, a conscious revival of 'stately' classicism began, inspired by the work of Robert Adam. The beginning of an Adam revival was at first seen mainly in interior decoration, part of a rejection of late nineteenth-century interiors as 'dark' and 'cluttered'. The

[103] Burnet & Campbell: Athenaeum Theatre, Buchanan St, Glasgow (1891)

[104] J.J. Burnet: Atlantic Chambers, Argyle St, Glasgow (1899–1900)

[105] Lion Chambers, Hope Street, Glasgow (1904–7)

James Salmon experimented with a 'Scottish' skyscraper style inspired not by America but by 'the old rough-cast castle' of the Scottish Renaissance. In 1904-7, Salmon and Gillespie designed and built Lion Chambers, a tall office block combined with top floor artists' studios, using the patented (Hennebique) concrete frame and panel construction, to allow maximum accommodation on a tiny site: the building measured 90-feet high, but only 33 by 46 feet in area. Unlike real tower houses, the walls were astonishingly thin: a mere four inches. This startling attempt to devise an 'artistic' type of high office block, with overtones of cultural nationalism, echoed the earlier work of Sullivan in America.

[106] Alhambra Theatre, Glasgow (1911)

Burnet's later work further 'stripped' Beaux Arts down to an architecture of bold, simple shapes, where the influence of Thomson was more emphatic. Burnet's McGeoch building, in Glasgow (1905), and Forsyth's, in Edinburgh (1906), used gridded façades within overall Baroque compositions. From 1910–11, his designs became even more austere. In two commercial buildings, the Kodak building, London (1910) and the Wallace Scott Institute, Cathcart (1913), the main façade comprises a simplified colonnade, flanked at Wallace Scott by massive pylons and at Kodak by vertical openings crowned by a huge cornice. In the Alhambra Theatre, the debt to Thomson was made clearer. The design was punched with vertical slits linked by a deep, canopied-eaves colonnade, and surmounted by oriental domes.

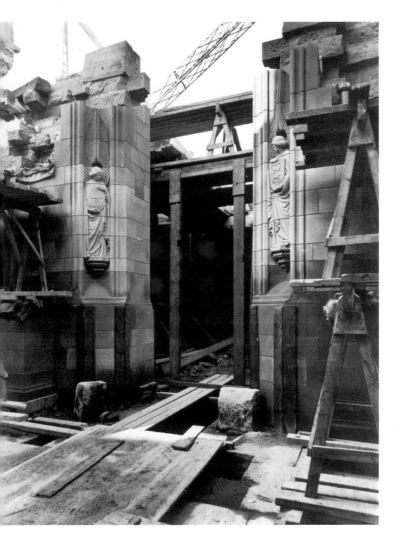

[107] **Building the Scottish National War Memorial (1924–7)**

After the First World War, the older tendencies were continued: the cult of the house, social housing reform, archaic monumentality, and neo-Romanesque church architecture. Just as before, the basic inspiration was Scots Renaissance classicism. However, the previous ideal of a 'national style' took on a critical edge. For the first time, comparisons were made with English architecture. In 1928, Lorimer criticised the awarding of commissions to English designers. Still, this did not reflect any separatist political tendency. One of Lorimer's greatest works was his own public monument to imperial warfare: the Scottish National War Memorial. Lorimer brilliantly converted an eighteenth-century barracks into a massive, nave-like space (the Hall of Honour), with tall octagonal columns, round-headed windows and a Falkland Palace-like bay arrangement. Attached at the centre was the Shrine, a significantly neo-Romanesque apse.

alternative was an austere 'whiteness'. The main 'Adams' movement in Scotland first focused on genuine Adam houses: schemes such as Wright & Mansfield's work at Haddo House (1880). A more scholarly stage was reached in Sir James Miller's commissioning of John Kinross from 1891 to remodel Manderston into an 'Adams'/Louis XVI showpiece. The Adam Revival was extended into the beginnings of a New Town Revival in 1904, when the 4th Marquess of Bute bought and re-ordered in Adam style 5 Charlotte Square, Edinburgh. Rowand Anderson's addition of a tall dome in 1886–7 to Adam's main university façade was part of a general neo-eighteenth-century trend, and there followed a rash of ever calmer 'public'-style buildings such as R.S. Lorimer's New Library, St Andrews (1907–8).

The 1920s and early 1930s saw Sellars' revival of Thomson further intensified. The most powerful example came, predictably, from Burnet's firm at Adelaide House, a large commercial block in London (1920–5) by Thomas S. Tait who became a partner in 1919. Now the emphasis was less on skyscrapers and more on monumental city blocks, as huge plots were bought and developed.

This American trend towards designing office blocks as freestanding buildings was also taken forward outwith Burnet's firm, particularly in Glasgow. The prototype was James Miller's Union Bank headquarters, St Vincent Street (1924–7), and it was developed in a Beaux-Arts/neo-Thomson phase in 1920s Glasgow by Wylie, Wright & Wylie's Scottish Legal Life Assurance Society headquarters (1927–31). The steel-framed front façade echoed the Burnet tradition in its general arrangement of flanking pylons, central colonnade and deep-set eaved windows.

During the 1930s, the modernity of Beaux Arts planning was applied to social building projects such as schools like E.G. Wylie's cross-shaped, red-brick Hillhead High (1928–31), with its corridors open to the winds. In hospital planning, also, the emphasis on fresh air, sunlight and dispersed layouts remained strong. Burnet, Tait & Lorne's Paisley Infectious Diseases Hospital (from 1933) had parallel blocks, while James Miller & Son's Auxiliary Hospital and Convalescent Home, Canniesburn (1937–8) comprised a single group with wings. On urban sites, new American-inspired concepts of controlling the spread of infection by technology rather than cross-ventilation prompted a planning trend back towards concentration in steel-framed multi-storey blocks such as Wylie's Glasgow Dental Hospital of 1927–31, which again echoed the Burnet formula of pylons flanking a framed façade.

The stately, stripped classicism of Beaux Arts social provision was counteracted in the 1930s by a new, whimsical architecture of leisure. Here, there was a powerful, American Beaux-Arts influence, transmitted through the medium of the cinema, especially in Glasgow. The cinema boom had begun as early as 1910: the Green's Playhouse cinema and dance-hall complex, opened in 1925 with 4400 seats, was then the largest in Europe. This was also a national phenomenon: many of the smallest burghs acquired their own picture houses. The late 1930s also saw ice-rinks, swimming-pools, cafés and bars with American chrome styling. In some industrial projects, too, a showy 'modernity' was aimed at: for instance, at Cornelius Armour's Luma Light Bulb Factory of 1936–8 [colour plate 31].

To many young designers, the Continental Modern Movement, like the cinema to the general public, provided an image of escape from the worthiness of Imperial Scotland. Young Edinburgh architects such as Basil Spence reacted against 'tradition'. In 1933 he and William Kininmonth joined forces and designed Art Deco villas at Dick Place (1933: Kininmonth's own house) and Easter Belmont Road (1935). However, Spence also designed a Lorimerian villa at 6 Castlelaw Road (1932); then a 'moderne' concrete garage at Causewayside, Edinburgh (1933); a painted cottage-terrace at Dunbar (1934–5); and, finally, the spectacular Broughton Place (1935–8), a massive tower-house recalling Formakin. The key to their work was a new spirit of eclecticism, devoid of the socialist morality of Continental Modernism.

NATIONAL DWELLING TYPES

The main field for architect-designed mass housing was now no longer in the private sphere, but in the field of public social housing. As house building became a major industry, architects were inevitably squeezed out. Despite calls, especially in the east, to continue with stone, harled brickwork became standard; but the shortage of bricklayers also led to increasing

[108] Jordanhill College, Glasgow (1913–22)

[109] Tollcross School, Edinburgh (1911–13)
The Glasgow Exhibition of 1911 focused further interest on the possibilities of the national style for educational buildings, a move away from mainstream classicism. H. & D. Barclay's Jordanhill College has something of a St Machar's-like drama within a Franco-Scottish composition, and J.A. Carfrae's Tollcross School recalls the garden front of Pinkie [14].

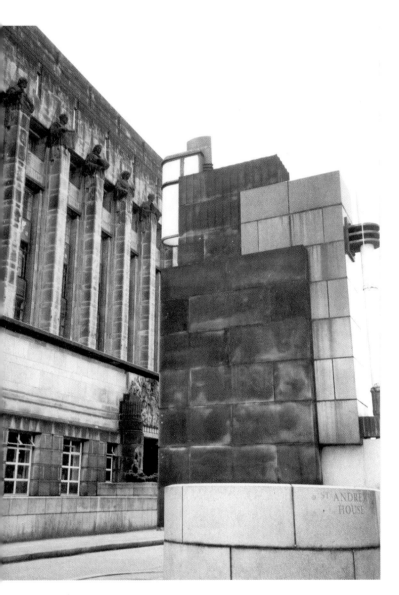

[110] St Andrews House, Edinburgh (1936–9)

The climax of the revived devotion to Thomson was the new governmental complex at St Andrew's House, designed by Thomas Tait. A dramatic site on the edge of Calton Hill was exploited with a pyramidal, terraced composition; the entrance front was dominated by a massive central block with sculpture-crowned piers. In 1934, Tait described the St Andrew's House proposal: 'The design is simple and sculpturesque rather than decorative, but carried out with that strength and refinement expressive of present-day sentiments … A direct scientific approach … beauty, dignity, and refined simplicity.'

reliance on concrete blockwork building. There were also experiments with steel houses and mass concrete construction. But there were now implications for dwelling types. State intervention in housing was combined with imposition of hygienic standards, especially through density reduction and promotion of cottage garden-suburbs. High costs and tenant opposition soon led to revived large-scale building of smaller flats, in two-storey 'four in a block' units, or three-storey tenements. This compromise solution of lower-density flats, based on long-established private patterns in smaller burghs, had already emerged in the first completed post-war municipal scheme, Logie in Dundee, built in 1919–20 under James Thomson's direction.

With the success of the Empire Exhibition's modernity and 'efficiency' what happened to Traditionalism? The collectivism of the 1930s had given importance to the ordinary dwelling and the ideal of social community, and this became a battleground for socialist Modernism and 'organic' Traditionalism. The 'openness' of municipal housing schemes was bound to be at odds with Traditionalist notions of 'organic' small burghs where 'the big rubs shoulders with the small, and all stand in a warm and friendly neighbourliness'. In new architectural design during the 1930s, two tendencies emerged. The first formed part of the typical northern European search for a 'national' type of small dwelling. The second branch of 1930s Traditionalist housing design had much greater consequences for future housing provision, being concerned with dwellings in linked groups, like the small burgh. It continued Geddes' emphasis on enclosed rather than open space, and thus implicitly opposed the open planning of Continental Modernist urbanism.

As before, the design of new housing inspired by the past naturally linked up with the aim of preserving old buildings. Geddes' advocacy of 'conservation of the historic heritage' was progressively developed into the beginnings of state-sponsored 'listing'. In 1931, the National Trust for Scotland was founded, and soon extended its work from landscape to building conservation. Before long, the new 1930s nationalist rhetoric concerned itself with the whole question of Edinburgh Old Town. However, the demands of the 1930 Housing Act for slum-

[111] 'Empirex', Glasgow (1938)

The height of Beaux-Arts modernity was reached at the Glasgow Empire Exhibition (or 'Empirex') of 1938. In the midst of all of the hedging around the issue of old versus new came the opportunity and the necessity to lay Scotland's architectural cards on the table. The overall architectural theme of the exhibition was not Continental Modernism, but a simplified Beaux Arts laid out on axial lines, like a planned town. Amongst these 'technically efficient' ranks of exhibition pavilions were islands of romanticism, such as the re-run of the 'clachan' exhibit from 1911, with its thatched house and painted castle. Scotland's 'national identity' was now firmly identified as a landscape issue. **[see also colour plates 32, 33]** The imagery of the 'Auld Toon' had acquired a negative reputation through writers like A.J. Cronin and Lewis Grassic Gibbon.

Modernity's emphasis on asymmetrical 'dynamism' was expressed through the 300-foot Tower of Empire, a symbolic observation point rising from a restaurant building at the summit of Bellahouston Park. The Tower was built using the same system as the other buildings: steel-framing covered in corrugated asbestos sheeting. The end of 'Empirex' marked a recovery of confidence, both in Glasgow and across the whole nation. Lord Provost Patrick Dollan pronounced that 'the exhibition has taught us all a finer and more colourful way of living, and that it is possible in Glasgow to educate and enjoy ourselves without drabness and greyness'.

clearance soon shifted conservation fears from Old Edinburgh to the smaller burghs. The focus of concern was Fife, where the NTS was already (in 1932) beginning its restoration of Culross. In 1937, Stirling-Maxwell described small burgh houses as 'precious records of the national life'. But the most significant boost to this campaign came in 1936 with the publication of a polemical pamphlet, *A Plea for Scotland's Architectural Heritage*, by Scotland's premier inter-war preserver, the 4th Marquess of Bute.

Bute's architectural 'crusade' was concerned not with country houses but with small burgh dwellings. Where his father, in Anderson's words, was 'never out of the mortar tub', the 4th Marquess made his mark in conservation by political lobbying and by anonymously 'mothballing' threatened buildings such as Loudon Hall, Ayr. Bute began a campaign to offset the effects of slum clearance, by making a record of old burgh houses and convincing the government to agree to a burgh survey. Bute then employed Ian Lindsay (who had worked with the National Trust at Culross and Dunkeld) to carry out the survey. Over the next two years 92 burghs were inventorised. To complement these efforts, the Scottish National Buildings Record was set up in 1941, under Bute (as

[112] 'Louisville House', No. 4 Louisville Avenue, Aberdeen (1975)

[113] Morningside Gardens, Aberdeen (early 20th-c. bungalow development)
In domestic architecture, although the private sector still built occasional groups of tenements, the falling cost of land and the wider availability of motor transport encouraged the dominance of a new solution: the bungalow. In Aberdeen, a broad monumentalism took forward a classical tradition in single storey house design. The more whimsical, colonial bungalow with veranda was rarely seen.

[114] Ian Lindsay (1906–66)

During the 1950s, Traditionalism as a movement of new architecture was largely channelled into preservation. Ian Lindsay became a leader of that grouping, carrying out conservationist schemes in burghs such as Culross, Dunkeld and Inveraray, creating the painted black and white image that we take for granted today and that became associated across the board with 'heritage'. But Lindsay made a far greater impact, between 1945 and 1966, in the field of government 'listing'. Here, he was charged with carrying out a nationwide inventory. At first, there was a continuing stress on small burgh architecture. Soon, however, the growing influence of art history began to change the emphasis towards listing the works of named architects. The preservationists became an avant garde of the modern heritage movement, apparently opposing, from within government, the general enthusiasm for reconstruction.

chairman) and George Scott-Moncrieff (as secretary). Its aim, in Scott-Moncrieff's words, was above all to record the 'modest homes of the people'.

THE GROWTH OF PLANNING

The loss of life and economic cost of the First World War dealt a huge blow to imperial Scotland's confident sense of national identity and material progress, yet the country remained relatively stable. Ideas of the 'national' in architecture were ever more people-based and focused on housing. In this expanding field, the government in 1915 had fatally compromised the private-rented sector with rent controls and the influential 1917 Royal Commission report (the Ballantyne Report) had popularised the notion that Scotland suffered an especially bad 'housing problem'. The way was clear for state intervention, eventually on a massive scale.

During the 1920s, the conflict between the two competing interpretations of 'national tradition' (classical continuity and Traditionalist golden age) died down. There were still sharp divergences, but by the later 1920s and early 1930s, the old preoccupation with 'national tradition' seemed backward-looking in comparison with Beaux-Arts modernity, which changed its focus from the commercialism of the 1920s to the social programmes and new popular building types of the 1930s. During this decade, the system of devolved government administration gained strength. Large spending programmes for mass housing began.

[115] Cruachan Dam Hydro scheme (1960–5)

The culmination of state-sponsored Traditionalism was located in the Highlands through the North of Scotland Hydro-Electric Board. Paradoxically, it was the Board's engineering works – which began at Loch Sloy (from 1946) and culminated in the Cruachan scheme (1960–5) – that made an impression on many Modernist architects. In 1952, Basil Spence declared that the dams recalled 'the magnificence of Roman architecture'. In the first big schemes, Sloy (1946–50) and Tummel-Garry (1947–53), H.O. Tarbolton designed the power stations themselves in a flat, boxy style similar to Fairlie's National Library. The next series of stations was commissioned from Shearer & Annand. Shearer became the most forceful designer-propagandist of Hydro architecture, and a vehement opponent of cosmopolitan Modernism's 'glassy, shadowless architecture'. His stations for the Affric project were squat, cubic and detailed in simplified classical fashion: at the largest, Fasnakyle (1952), Hew Lorimer sculpted low-relief panels of 'Celtic legends'. Shearer used locally quarried rubble for the stations, and built a 'model Highland village' of stone-built staff houses at Cannich, the first of several such schemes.

This was an obvious area for renewed Traditionalist rhetoric. In opposition to Americanism and, now, Continental Modernism, many architects began to give voice to a 'national re-awakening'. Ian C. Hannah's *The Story of Scotland in Stone* (1934) complained that 'the wide river of Scottish culture has for many days flowed in a course that has been well-nigh Jewish in its cosmopolitanism'. This prompted the emergence of a new generation of architects who hoped to modernise, but under a cloak of traditional architectural forms.

Although sixteenth- and seventeenth-century Scottish architecture was still the source of inspiration, this was to be boiled down into an 'essence' rather than direct quotations from Billings or MacGibbon and Ross. Now Mackintosh was hailed as herald of the new 'national' modernism. For public buildings, a flat-faced monumental classicism was favoured. For larger churches, too, there was a new tendency towards simplified classicism. In domestic buildings, including smaller churches, an elemental, harled simplicity, with massive, steep roofs, was preferred, clearly allied with small burgh collective architecture.

Traditionalism found a rich new outlet in public buildings. 'Empirex' had showcased the Highlands' scenic beauty, the plan was now to harness its natural resources. Following principles first laid down by the wartime Secretary of State (1941–5), Tom Johnston, the Scottish Office was to co-ordinate a programme of regeneration which would balance the needs of the industrial Lowlands for modernisation with those of the Highlands for the stemming of depopulation. There was to be planned social provision, and planned regional development through the building of new towns in the Lowlands, and a revitalisation of the Highlands through a huge hydro-electric programme.

Debates on what form the new architecture of social necessity should take became increasingly polarised between the Modern and the Traditional. The Moderns emphasised a left-leaning progressiveness, and the Traditionalists a 'national' ideal. Both, however, were unfailingly progressive in terms of standards. The new breed of Modernists demanded new 'community planning', based on international Modernist principles of building according to 'needs'. Some younger

Traditionalists, emerging from the patrician hierarchy of the Anderson generation, nevertheless wished for a new community architecture based on national examples.

ROBERT MATTHEW AND MODERNISM

In spite of its rhetoric of 'community', Traditionalism was still laden with patrician values and led by the aristocracy and their upper-middle-class architects. Other young architects were inspired instead by the socialist rhetoric of the Continental Modern Movement; the *ideas* of the international Modern Movement, rather than simply its appearance. At the heart of Continental Modernism was the notion that it was possible actually to solve social problems through a new kind of design approach, in which 'needs' would be integrated with the appearance of a building. The overall task was seen as facilitating the march of progress, which was more and

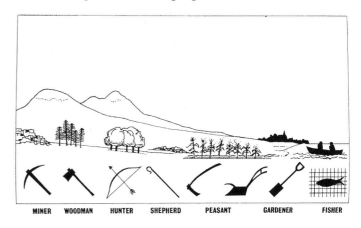

[116] Valley Section, 'A typical region'

The notion that entire cities and regions could be scientifically designed was, in Scotland, ultimately inspired by Patrick Geddes. Where Geddes had been concerned with Edinburgh, the focus of his successors' campaigns was Glasgow. More and more attention was devoted to debating the 'Glasgow problem', and arguing that it should be tackled by a combination of Modern redevelopment and satellite garden-city communities. In 1943 Patrick Abercrombie and Robert Matthew were asked to prepare a regional plan for the entire Clyde Valley, an echo of Geddes' celebrated 'Valley Section' (above). The plan took in both Glasgow and the areas in which satellite towns might be established. The planners envisaged an ambitious re-ordering of population and industry. Dense Glasgow would be 'overspilled' into planned new towns by declaring much of its suburban building land to be Green Belt, thus diverting building of new houses away from the city. In 1947, the first new town, East Kilbride, was designated.

HOSPITALS

We go to hospitals to get well. Dreary, inefficient buildings retard recovery, depressing the patient and hindering the nurse.

Lightness, freshness and good planning on an open site are minimum needs.

Royal Infirmary, Edinburgh

HOSPITAL, CZECHOSLOVAKIA

[117] 'Building Scotland' (1941)

The new 'Vernacular' was largely the brainchild of Matthew's partner, Alan Reiach. His ideas were expressed forcefully in his polemical book, written with Robert Hurd, Building Scotland. Arguing through oppositions of 'good' and 'bad' photographs in the manner of Pugin's Contrasts, they advocated a revival in new architecture of the 'homely and spacious' values embodied in old buildings. In a reversal of Pugin, 19th-century Gothic was 'bad' and new Functionalism 'good'.

more associated with socialism. In 1960, Frank Walker wrote that 'both the international socialist movement and the modern architectural movement … are expressions in different fields of the new scientific outlook on life.'

This 'scientific' Modernism focused on Scotland's decaying industrial heartland, and proposed its replacement by planned communities. In accordance with formulas marked out by the International Congresses of Modern Architecture (CIAM), the new philosophy emphasised provision 'for all': dwellings in residential areas segregated from industrial and other functions, provided with open space, sunlight and integrated social facilities: these communities might even be in separate planned towns. There was also a new concept of unadorned buildings arranged in free, open patterns, sometimes incorporating high towers to provide a degree of monumentality.

The driving force behind Modernism was a huge desire to sweep away the fusty old world of density and decay, and to replace it with something bright and new. Within Scotland, these demands cut across the existing debate between the garden city and tenement revival advocates. As a compromise, the Department of Housing for Scotland encouraged municipalities to build more unified and open-planned schemes of tene-

ments, such as the grandiose classicism of Port Glasgow Town Council's tenement projects or Aberdeen City Architect Albert Gardner's curved, metal-windowed courtyard group at Rosemount Square (from 1938).

A more radical break came with the emergence of Robert Matthew as a force in Scottish architecture. Matthew had qualified in 1931 and spent two years in his father's office, Lorimer & Matthew. For the would-be international Modernist in the 1930s, the first duty was to address the housing problem. In a prize-winning project of 1935 for urban redevelopment, he proposed not tenement-height blocks, but ten-storey slabs with 'community' facilities such as nursery schools and health centres. On the basis of this work, Matthew was engaged by the government in 1936 as an assistant architect, but was soon put in charge of the department.

Robert Matthew's growing international status ensured that the Modernist view rapidly became the establishment view, and began to shape post-war Scottish reconstruction. However, quite typically in Scotland, his own interpretation of Modern Movement ideology overlapped in some ways with the 'national' concerns of late Traditionalism. He called for a 'National Movement' in Scotland, an evocation in 'contempo-

rary work' of 'the strong and almost unique character of Braid Scots in architecture'. Matthew attempted to broker a compromise between Modernism and Traditionalism through the idea of the 'organic', claiming that people had been alienated from architecture. He agreed with the Traditionalists in calling for the revival of stone building, but in rationalistic terms as Scotland's 'basic building material'.

The Second World War's centralised planning chimed in with Modernism, and the state-socialism that followed encouraged its adherents. Scottish housing output, in the 1950s, would be dominated by public authorities to an extent far exceeding that of any other developed country, East or West. Even in the 1960s nearly 80 per cent of output was publicly built (compared to, for example, 3 per cent in West Germany or 0.3 per cent in Belgium).

After the war, the materials crisis worsened. By 1947, the non-traditional proportion of total Scottish permanent housing output had reached two-thirds. Matthew was closely involved with this campaign: in 1945 he designed type plans for the building of cottages using prefabricated timber sections made in Sweden. In 1949 he commented that 'we are still suffering from a sense of shock at the sight of an aluminium prefabricated house trundling along the highway'. However in the west, Sam Bunton, who established himself during the war as a co-ordinating figure in prefabricated social building, claimed in 1953 that 'Timber and brick is a prehistoric method of building.'

After the war, the gap between 'national' Traditionalism and 'international' Modernity began to break down, largely through the withering of Traditionalism as a force. Some architects, such as Steel Maitland, called themselves 'unrepentant Traditionalists', but on the whole there was an acceptance that modern society needed Modernism not nationalist antiquarianism. The last redoubt of the Traditionalists was, predictably, the small burghs and the rural dwellings. The shift towards more Modern ideas in small-burgh infill schemes began at Basil Spence's Dunbar fishermen's housing scheme (1949–52), with its rubble and harl walling, metal windows and forestair-like concrete balconies.

Among Scottish architects, there was around 1960 a general feeling of optimism that the welfare-state standards defined in the 1940s were now, at last, being provided for all through the medium of Modern architecture. Architects were building a 'new Scotland' for 'the people' not just for the wealthy. This triumph of the avowedly internationalist Modern Movement was to prove short-lived, however, especially in the very area of community planning.

[118] Turnhouse Airport, Edinburgh (1954–6)
Robert Matthew's first commission in private practice, Turnhouse Airport Terminal, was a sharp contrast to Kininmonth's contemporary Renfrew design, with its flamboyant arches. Planned from 1952 and built in 1954–6, Turnhouse was a low, asymmetrical group, steel-framed (with welded portal frames) to allow extension, and faced with Auchinlea sandstone and brick on the base, and mahogany cladding above in the manner of Alvar Aalto's Finnish Modernism. A concern for Vernacular was also evident in Matthew's own series of Highland power stations, including Lochay (1957–9), and Cashlie (1957–60), where Matthew used unadorned wall planes of rubble. The climax of Matthew's work in power stations was the single-chimneyed Longannet (opened 1966).

Matthew even attempted to bring Traditionalist continuity to the multi-storey block. By the mid-1950s, the tall tower or slab had become perhaps the most universally recognised and exclusive symbol of architectural Modernity. Matthew's Queen's College Dundee tower (1958–61) added a vertical punctuation in a 'modern idiom' to Perth Road, faced in rubble and timber, a symbol of the Modernist/Traditional compromise attempted in his work.

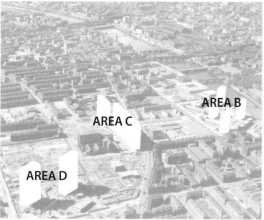

[119] Aerial view of Hutchesontown (Gorbals), Glasgow (from 1956)

Hutchesontown-Gorbals was one of the biggest Comprehensive Development Areas in the UK. One site (Area 1956) was rebuilt using four-storey, tenement-scale maisonettes. Area B was allocated to Robert Matthew (1958–64; with Ian Arnott and John Paterson); Area C to Basil Spence (1960–6; with Charles Robertson); and Area D (1961–8) to the experimental state agency, the Scottish Special Housing Association. Matthew designed 18-storey towers and lower blocks laid out on a north-south axis, disregarding existing street alignments.

Around 1960, there was a general belief that the world could be a better place, in a future of mass contentedness in designed communities. Modernism in architecture was only part of this widespread faith in progress and reconstruction in the face of war and crisis. The 1960s saw the final decline of heavy industry, but also the building up of a 'cleaner' economic base, driven by the 'white heat' of new technology. People were demanding reconstruction across the board: in housing, in education and in road-building. Yet the affluence created by this mass effort of reconstruction, instead of encouraging 'community' seemed in the end to foster individualism. People soon began to question assumptions about 'how we shall live in the future'. The basis of planning had been delayed gratification, and a satisfaction about being part of a community effort. Soon, people would want to shape their own futures.

For the moment, the effort of reconstruction required planning above all else. Most infrastructural functions within government were in 1962 gathered into a single body, the Scottish Development Department. The idea was for the state to create wealth through spending on large-scale projects. A series of grandiose plans was prepared, including the 'National Plan for Scotland' of 1966. A new optimism about the Highlands led in 1965 to the establishment of a development agency with industrial investment powers: the Highlands and Islands Development Board. Confidence in the future of motor transport was high, and an accelerated road-building drive was a key part of planned modernisation. The showpiece was the elegant Forth Road Bridge (1958–64, Mott Hay & Anderson/Sir G. Scott).

In terms of architecture, the focus had been on new 'communities' such as East Kilbride, but it would soon turn back on the cities and the idea of 'regeneration' of existing settlements.

This regeneration was at first awesome in scale, envisaging the virtual rebuilding of cities. The first burgh to embark on a planned Modern redevelopment drive was Paisley, but the focus of most attention was, inevitably, Glasgow. Here, the planners proposed to channel slum-clearance into twenty-nine 'Comprehensive Development Areas' (CDAs), much of whose population would be 'overspilled', out of the city. The most prestigious of these, Hutchesontown/Gorbals [119], was allocated to a range of designers.

Through the necklace of CDA clearance was to be threaded nothing less than a full-scale motorway [133]. The north and west flanks were begun in 1965, including a high-level Clyde crossing, the Kingston Bridge. Glasgow's mid-1960s combination of area redevelopment, new tower blocks and road schemes seemed to promise a full-scale realisation in Scotland of Modernist urbanism, presaged in Futurist fantasies of the 1920s. Architects were warned that they would have to 'think big' if they were to take part in the adventure of Modernism. But 'architecture' – in the 'artistic' sense – was gradually squeezed out.

As Modernism arrived, it came under threat from the housing lobby. From 1961, the Glasgow planners' formula was challenged by 'housers' opposed to overspill and consequent loss of political power and 'Second City' prestige. The idea of Glasgow as an important 'world city' was deeply ingrained, and, to stem the flow of population, the Housing Committee began to build high and fast: on gap sites, as and when they came up. The end of this campaign came with a colossal group of steel-framed tower and slab blocks designed by Sam Bunton and built by the city's direct labour at Red Road, Balornock (1962–9).

Many big blocks were also designed as 'package deals' by contractors like Wimpey or Crudens: for instance, Crudens's ten twenty-storey slab blocks at Sighthill (1963–9). In the process, architects were pushed aside. Even Robert Matthew was sacked from two sites, at Springburn and Royston, because he had pressed for 'comprehensive' development of a wider area. Despite the astonishing success of Glasgow's schemes in terms of providing new houses, many Modern designers – having been frozen out – began to say that these high blocks were not properly 'Modern' at all. The Glasgow architect Isi Metzstein declared – echoing Ruskin – that a distinction now had to be made 'between architecture and building'.

International Modernism, at the moment of its triumph, was beginning to break up. In Europe, critics rejected the Modernist view of 'community' as crude. Alongside this was a tendency, led by architects such as Le Corbusier and Louis Kahn, to present a new 'sculptural' Modernism which emphasised buildings' appearance. John L. Paterson of RMJM argued that 'we have to create in our existing cities an image or images which reflect the character of that city'. When working as job architect for Hutchesontown 'B', Paterson suggested that the tower blocks' elevations should be faced with broken bottles, as a symbol of the 'social reality' of the Gorbals. It was not long before 'back greens' and 'stair heids' were being idealised in opposition to the 'lonely isolation' of tower blocks.

In 1955, Morris & Steedman attempted to devise 'a specifically Scottish house', but this search for the 'national' took its inspiration from the houses of Neutra, Johnson and other post-war Modernists in America, which Morris and Steedman had visited in the mid-1950s. Their first commission, the Tomlinson house ('Avisfield', 1956–7), Edinburgh, was constructed of stone and painted brick, with a 'Scottish' rubble wall and a 'secret' courtyard garden.

The central ideas of these private commissions were soon tried in public housing, not in individual units, but in the form of dense, low layouts, sometimes described as 'cluster' or 'carpet'. Sociological justification was provided by Robert Matthew's Edinburgh University Housing Research Unit, set up in 1959. The Unit concentrated on 'the factors which turn a group of dwellings into a community'. Its first building scheme was a group of 45 patio houses at Prestonpans (1962).

The most comprehensive realisation of this low, dense pattern of community design was achieved at a New Town: Cumbernauld. Here, planning reacted against the 'individualism' of East Kilbride's housing types by at first proposing a compact urban mass around a hill-top town centre. The terraced cottages and low flats that were eventually built were not

[120] Port Murray, Maidens (1960–3)
A solution to the new 'problem' of mass housing was at first worked out, paradoxically, in the field of private housing. A series of innovative small houses was produced by Peter Womersley. He had previously designed 'Farnley Hey' (1952–4), in Northern England, with an open-plan layout on a steep wooded site. 'High Sunderland' (1956–7), built for the textile designer Bernat Klein, was later planned around two courtyards with striking contrasts of colour and materials. The most spectacular of Womersley's houses was at Port Murray, where he devised a romantic cliff-top composition in the long tradition stretching from Culzean to Thomson's Craig Ailey and beyond.

[121] Cumbernauld Town Centre, Phase One (1963–7)
Whilst the housing at Cumbernauld increasingly reflected old Scottish planned town precedents, the Town Centre recalled the Enlightenment ambition of Robert Adam's own contribution to town planning. Cumbernauld's Town Centre 'megastructure' was designed to combine every single function of town life, and was even penetrated by a full-scale highway.

dissimilar to East Kilbride, but here there were much denser layouts and hard landscaping which sought to reflect a Scottish national 'tradition': rows of cottages with steep roofs, and groups of flat-roofed and split-level houses such as Seafar 2 (1961–3). Around these was planted a new 'forest', designed to evoke the settings of housing in Finland or Norway.

The megastructural tendency and the concern to strip away architecture to its 'essence' also pointed to renewed concern with 'form'. Abroad, Le Corbusier moved towards a more personalised, even eccentric appearance for his buildings: Isi Metzstein praised this work's 'monumentality without rhetoric'. Also influential was the work of Louis Kahn; in Scotland his rejection of rationalist design in favour of the symbolism of 'form' was expressed in William Whitfield's Glasgow University Library (1965–81). This project's towered shape masked the bulk of the 'warehouse for books' required by the Librarian and provided a typically Glaswegian monumental landmark.

The most consistent Scottish champion of this 'formal' architecture in the 1960s was Peter Womersley. Womersley designed a series of public buildings, conceived as pieces of concrete 'sculpture'. Now that structure could be dealt with by consultants, the architect was free to create whatever outward form he/she chose. Womersley's commissions included the massive first phase of Roxburgh County Buildings, with tower (1966–8); and the studio for Bernat Klein at High Sunderland (1969–72) with open-plan interior, externally articulated by deep, horizontally projecting edge beams. Most complex was the Nuffield Transplantation Surgery Unit at the Western General Hospital, Edinburgh. The unit (designed 1963, built 1965–8) comprised a low ward unit with jutting stair tower, lobby and office wing.

In opposition to the preoccupation with form, another feature of 1960s' architecture was an almost clinical rationalism. In the field of public architecture, there was an emphasis on precise construction. This tendency became especially associated with RMJM's Edinburgh office when John Richards took Matthew's Functionalism a stage further by removing the Traditionalist element – the rubble cladding of Queen's College tower – from the equation. In its place, he developed an architecture of low ranges faced in precise dry-cladding: 'buildings you could put up in clean overalls, rather than grubbing around on a muddy building site.' The first to be built was the initial phase of the new University of Stirling (developed 1966–73) [126].

The Centre's designer, Geoffrey Copcutt, conceived the building as a 'nine-level package accommodating most of the commercial, civic, cultural and recreational uses for a population of 70,000 … a single citadel-like structure nearly half a mile long … a drive-in town centre'. In 1967, the American Institute of Architects awarded Cumbernauld the prestigious R.S. Reynolds Memorial Award for Community Architecture, as 'the most significant current contribution to the art and science of urban design in the Western world'. Cumbernauld, they proclaimed, was 'designed for the millennium': 'the dreams of the 1920s and 1930s are being built on a hill near Glasgow'.

[122] St Peter's, Cardross (1959–66)
Cumbernauld Town Centre was a spectacular 'one-off', but many architects were deeply impressed with its complex grouping of layered functions within a single structure. Gillespie, Kidd & Coia began a series of educational commissions influenced by this 'sectional' planning. Reacting against older layouts with corridors and wings, their new megastructural pattern grouped teaching or residential accommodation around communal spaces. The most significant was St Peter's Seminary at Cardross (project architect: Isi Metzstein), a courtyard complex on a steep site (like Corbusier's La Tourette, 1953–60) with an existing 19th-century

Baronial house as the focus. The two main elements were a stepped-section accommodation block with a chapel and refectory below ranges of study-bedrooms, and a library and lecture block jutting out over woodland.

[123] Area 'C', Hutchesontown, Glasgow (1960–6)

The most visually stylish of all Scottish images of urban massing was Basil Spence's design for Area 'C' of the Hutchesontown redevelopment in Glasgow (project architect: Charles Robertson; demolished 1993). He grouped the 400 dwellings required into a line of 20-storey towers, which were aligned into two long slab blocks by linked by 'garden slabs' on alternate floors, each intended to provide sheltered open space for the adjacent four dwellings.

[124] Maiden Lane, London (1976–81)

The influence of Cumbernauld Town Centre as the 'canonical megastructure' was long-lasting, especially in 'urban hot spots' where there was 'little alternative to a decked development'. At Maiden Lane, London, the Scottish architects Gordon Benson and Alan Forsyth developed a miniaturised megastructure and dense housing solution.

[125] St Paul's Church, Glenrothes (1956–7)

Gillespie Kidd & Coia experimented with innovations for low-cost churches in new housing areas. The first of these was St Paul's Church in Glenrothes New Town (architect in charge, Andy MacMillan) – a wedge-shaped church built of white painted common brick. All the ingredients of the later 'Coia style' were there, such as 'sectional' top-lighting of a type seen in the work of Arne Jacobsen and others, and sweeping walls with small, neo-Mackintosh windows. From about 1960, all Gillespie, Kidd & Coia's churches were designed in this Late Modernist manner. St Bride's, East Kilbride (1963–4) contained a single, rectangular windowless space, lit through timber spars in the roof. By the mid-1960s, all Gillespie, Kidd & Coia's churches had adopted centralised, non-rectangular plans, reflecting the new people-centred liturgy.

The most atmospheric of these was Sacred Heart Church, Cumbernauld (1964) which was lit through coloured glass. Many of the firm's more extravagant designs also proved problematical: the Roman Catholic Church demolished some of their most daring buildings, including St Benedict's Drumchapel and the tower of St Bride's, citing insurmountable structural or maintenance problems. Building defects in these churches and elsewhere in some of the most 'architectural' designs of the age were later linked to a general 'failure' of Modernism.

[126] John Richards (RMJM): University of Stirling (1966–73)

[127]   **Provost Ross's House, Aberdeen in 1950, with crumbling roof (right)**

[128]   **After restoration (1978)**

With the rise of conservation, Aberdeen's 1952 City Plan had recognised the need to preserve the 'authentic old world atmosphere' of Old Aberdeen along with certain historic buildings throughout the city such as Provost Ross's House or Skene's Lodging, which was embedded in the municipal piazza around St Nicholas House.

THE 1970S: CONSERVATION AND CONTINUITY

By the end of the 1960s, Scotland had undergone a quite traumatic phase of reconstruction with all the upheaval that involved. Gradually, under the weight of all the certainties about the bold march into the future, cracks began to appear. The grandiose, pseudo-scientific 'solutions' favoured by teams of architects, planners, sociologists and economists began to be questioned. As a result, the status of planning began to decline sharply in the late 1960s and through the 1970s. This was a profound loss of faith that occurred in varying degrees in most western countries. Some said that the entire Modernist ideal of progress, through mass provision of new buildings, was flawed. Megastructure became a symbol of mechanistic crudity: the building of Burke & Martin's St James Centre (1964–70), containing a car park, hotel, shopping centre and offices, was strongly opposed by Edinburgh's growing conservation movement. The entire focus of architecture now shifted to 'place' and to 'heritage'.

Conservation provided the ideal antidote to redevelopment. Mainstream Modernism had made various concessions to old buildings and specific places: for example, the Glasgow Inner Ring Road was depressed in a cutting at Charing Cross and a 'bridge street structure' proposed in order to maintain the 'canyon' of Sauchiehall Street. Nevertheless old buildings and preservation had remained peripheral considerations.

In the 1970s the old gradually came to be valued more highly than the new. Conservation 'won' a victory over redevelopment. Ian Lindsay's advisory lists now became an apparatus of state control, and Robert Matthew, erstwhile redeveloper of George Square, was appointed conservation adviser to the Secretary of State. In 1974, Matthew blocked demolition of Mackintosh's Martyrs School, reminding the Secretary of State that 'we are surely past the stage when a unique part of this country's most valuable architectural heritage has to disappear on account of urban road works.' The 'precious' curve of the mighty ring road was altered for the sake of a redundant school. It was only a matter of time before the same tactics of heritage value could be applied to any historic building, including the city's most basic form – the tenement.

Along with growing opposition to the completion of the M8, in Glasgow, a new formula of housing 'rehabilitation'

emerged in a tenement improvement scheme at Taransay Street, Govan (from 1971). This community-based pattern was made the basis of the 1974 Housing Act, and by the early 1980s, the city was absorbing half of all Scottish housing improvements expenditure. For architects, this meant that 're-hab' took over the vast majority of their work and that the prestige of the old also dramatically affected the few new commissions.

Increasingly, there were attempts to distance new buildings from mainstream Modernism. There was a new concern with historical 'context'. Some architects used strong colours and chunky shapes adopted by 1970s' shop designers. Examples included Edwin Johnston & Nicholas Groves-Raines's 1971 White House Visitor Centre, Stirling [129]. Some late-Modernist schemes sought to reduce apparent bulk, as in the stepped sections of Michael Laird & Partners' Royal Bank Computer Centre, Edinburgh (1978) or James Parr's General Accident headquarters at Pitheavlis, near Perth (1982–3). In Aberdeen, the Town House Extension (1975, by City Architect Tom Watson) [75] attempted to remain 'in keeping' with granite. An easier way to re-visit the Vernacular architecture of the 1950s and 1960s was worked out by architects such as Wheeler & Sproson at Dysart, a historic burgh in Fife. Eventually, however, even Vernacular went too far. In 1982, Charles McKean lamented the loss of urban 'monumentality' caused

[129] Johnston & Groves-Raines: Visitor Centre, Stirling (1971)

by 'Neukery … a transitory, neo-vernacular fishing-village imagery' which has 'now started to invade our major cities'.

As before, in the age of Adam, eclecticism permitted a reassessment of national styles. But now 'national' no longer meant Baronial. Two tendencies stood out in the 1980s: the powerful 'neo-Baronial' of Ian Begg, and the Mackintosh Revival, led by Gillespie, Kidd & Coia. Begg's work comprised few but extremely prominent buildings which revived the Traditionalism of 1950s hydro designs (on which Begg had worked). The grandest of these projects was the Scandic Crown Hotel (1988–9), in the Edinburgh Old Town. This was treated as a picturesque composition, with a massive Holyrood-style tower as a corner feature. Similar in appearance, and even more controversial amongst fellow architects, was the St Mungo Museum of Religion, Glasgow (1990–3) [135].

The Mackintosh Revival was – by contrast – widely taken up. Mackintosh, of course, in one influential reading had been seen as a 'pioneer' of the Modern Movement so it was not such a huge task to bring his work back into public favour along with a general reassessment of Modernism. However, the revived Mackintosh was not the sensuous designer of curvilinear plant-like forms, nor the Traditionalist admirer of MacGibbon and Ross, but the late Mackintosh of the Chinese Room grids and the Art School west wing.

REGENERATION AND HERITAGE

City regeneration started in 1976 when the seventh New Town, Stonehouse, was abruptly cancelled and its resources were directed into 'GEAR' (Glasgow Eastern Area Renewal). The

[130] **Edinburgh International Conference Centre (1993–5)**
The 1980s saw a revival in the prestige of new building as Scotland participated in an international movement: Postmodernism.

Which are the Scottish Postmodern buildings? In Glasgow, Elder & Cannon designed the Bank of Pakistan (1981) in Sauchiehall Street, specifically recalling in a severe neo-Art Deco manner the Art Deco Gas showroom of 1935 which had

previously existed on the site. In Edinburgh, Campbell & Arnot's Saltire Court (1989–91) mixed-use, palace-fronted block seemed almost to reflect the ironic quality in Burnet. Indeed, it was the inherent irony in Postmodern classicism which guaranteed its short life. The whole episode seemed to culminate in the gigantic classical drum of Terry Farrell's Edinburgh International Conference Centre (1993–5).

[131] **Robinson College, Cambridge (1977–80)**

The key building in the Mackintosh revival was Gillespie, Kidd & Coia's Robinson College, Cambridge. Here the megastructural stepped section of Cardross was developed into a pattern of outer wall and internal street: 'more a fragment of the city than ... a college'. The outer walls were articulated with neo-Mackintosh lattice windows, while grid decoration was used extensively inside. The evocation of Mackintosh reached its climax in the library, a large space containing a freestanding,

three-storey timber structure recalling the iconic Art School library.

The debt to Mackintosh became clearer with successive stages of popularisation. Lattice patterns, grid decoration and stepped windows were to be seen everywhere. The Distillers headquarters, Edinburgh, by RMJM (1981–4) exemplified this new gridded neo-Mackintosh, with its boldly latticed stair towers. Andrew Merrylees's National Library Causewayside Building, Edinburgh (1985–7; extended 1994), took the pattern further with colliding gridded towers.

[132] **Page & Park: the Italian Centre, Glasgow (1988–94), with the City Chambers in the background**

city, above all else, was now seen as the appropriate arena for action: not 'clearance' but 'regeneration', driven by a certain nostalgia for pre-1914 community. The building type which seemed to sum up a pre-clearance, pre-Modern golden age was the tenement, previously the bugbear of housing reformers. Now the Modernist development replaced the tenement as the bogeyman of building: 'inhuman' in scale and imposed from above. The worsening image of the private car also enabled urban motorways to be condemned out of hand – even as car ownership increased as predicted.

Now in the city, there were to be small-scale 'interventions', following patterns established by existing old buildings. There was a renewed reverence for the picturesque, mixed-use neighbourhood, strongly advanced, for example, in the rhetoric of the Edinburgh Old Town Committee for Conservation and Renewal from 1984, which emphasised wealth creation and contained an implicit questioning of old-style planning. Informing these experiments was a new interest – obsession even – with 'place'. Modernism was regarded as a destroyer of community, a forward-looking, technology-driven juggernaut that would be stopped in its tracks by a new insistence on the ordinary and the past.

In terms of buildings, the first initiative was the regeneration of Glasgow's 'Merchant City', a run-down mixture of warehouses, offices and public buildings. From 1980, investment poured into the area, led by the SDA's City Centre Project. The

[133] Scott & Wilson, Kirkpatrick & Partners: frontispiece from *Report on a Highway Plan for Glasgow* (1965)

[134] below left: J. Swan: Glasgow Infirmary (*c.*1829)

To the right of the Infirmary (Robert Adam) lies Glasgow Cathedral (before demolition of the west towers) and the Barony Church (also designed by Robert Adam).

[135] above: St Mungo Museum, Glasgow (1990–3)

The high point of the heritage movement was reached at Cathedral Square in Glasgow. Here there was an attempt to re-establish a utopian burgh intimacy based on early 19th-century picturesque views of the city. The plan repudiated the 'Highway Plan for Glasgow' which had placed the Cathedral in a open Modernist setting. The new emphasis was on 'set-piece' planning, which related new buildings in an artfully organic manner. At the heart of the complex was the Cathedral, whose setting was reorganised by Page & Park in a scheme of 1984–1994. The same firm built sheltered housing, enclosing the east side of the new 'Cathedral Square'. Finally, Ian Begg designed the St Mungo Museum of Religion on the south side in a neo-Baronial style, further enclosing the area.

idea was to push the area upmarket by introducing groups of higher-income dwellings, and by 1990, 1143 houses had been built or converted in the area. The most complex achievement – by the developers, Kantel – was Ingram Square (1984–9), a street-block of 'artistic' regeneration, comprising ten separate sites designed by Elder & Cannon.

The climax of the Merchant City programme in the 1980s was the Italian Centre by Page & Park (completed 1992; extension 1993–4) a street-block of old warehouses converted into a mixed courtyard development 'where external restraint is set against a visually exciting and vibrant courtyard' [132].

THE 1990S

As we have seen, Postmodernism had a short life. It became a superficial style of labels and signs and the call soon went out for deeper meaning in architecture. Equally, there were concerns about Glasgow's image-led 'regeneration', in books like Sean Damer's *Glasgow: Going for a Song*. Was it all superficial? How could a thorough, meaningful architecture be arrived at? More controversially, were the prescriptions of the Moderns so thoroughly wrong?

These questions were raised in the second half of the 1980s, when John Richards praised the 'vigour' of 1950s Modernism, and Isi Metzstein attacked the 'polyfilla and plywood language of Postmodernism'. Underlying these attacks was perhaps a growing nostalgia for post-war community-based planning, as against the individualism of the 1980s. With this rejection of Postmodernism as 'applied decoration', we see a return – yet again – to an emphasis on the 'form' of buildings.

By the end of the 1980s some designers were simply giving their buildings a more obviously 'formal' appearance. Reiach & Hall's office block at 10 George Street (1993) aimed, according to its architect, both to give 'vigorous and honest expression' to 'steel frame and stone cladding'. This 'stone and steel style' then spread to commercial and public buildings, in something of a re-run of 1930s' office architecture. In spite of a new appreciation of Modernism, the approach to intervention in cities did not change radically, even allowing for the rejection of Postmodern 'pastiche'. Instead, architects attempted a more challenging interface with existing buildings, often citing the frank

interventions of earlier Modern architects such as Carlo Scarpa.

Page & Park's 1995–9 conversion of Mackintosh's Glasgow Herald building into an architecture centre (the 'Lighthouse') clamped a soaring new 'battery pack' of servant functions onto the old structure. In Edinburgh, Benson & Forsyth's extension of the Royal Museum of Scotland (1995–8) as the Museum of Scotland [**colour plate 39**] combined hand-picked stone cladding of a lovingly-detailed concrete structure with bold, episodic massing. The assertive urbanism of the exterior, and the megastructural section, demonstrated a new confidence, unconcerned with earlier qualms about 'flexibility'. A similar renewed interest in megastructure had been seen in the various competition entries for a National Gallery of Scottish Art (1994–8), particularly in the 'flowing space and volumes' of Elder & Cannon's entry.

[**136**] **Lanark County Buildings, Hamilton (1960–4)**
In spite of Modernism's explicit rejection of the past, many of its own buildings were subject to historical scrutiny. In 1993, for example, the Lanark County Buildings tower block was listed by Historic Scotland, and a Scottish branch of the international Modernist heritage group DOCOMOMO was set up, under the convenership of the author. The architectural historian Miles Glendinning has been behind much of the reassessment of Modernism, and he has also brought the period to the attention of today's architects, whose work he has surveyed. This reassessment of Modernism has led to a new interest among younger architects.

In social housing, there was a shift away from regeneration to 'city as monument' concerns to stop suburbanisation in the face of 'Brookside'-type developments of brick housing. In the search for an alternative to brick in new tenement design, a precedent had been set in 1984 by Ken MacRae's 'Tenement for the Twenty-first Century' (with McGurn Logan Duncan & Opfer) at Stratford Street, Maryhill, Glasgow. Once again in Scottish architecture, the main influence was Alexander Thomson, whose reputation was growing steadily. By the late 1980s and early 1990s, many Glasgow projects showed a similar concern for greater scale and dignity, and facing in stone or stone-like treatments. Elder & Cannon's Duke Street block (1992), with its Thomsonesque 'attic', also had split-level sections, with a severe front façade and a complex rear elevation of 'grander, more volumetric' living-rooms: it was built of beige brick laid in patterns in deference to the scale of channelled ashlar.

By the early 1990s, there was even an increasing demand for 'planning' as opposed to piecemeal infill. First was the Glasgow Crown Street Project, inspired by the Berlin IBA, whose 1992 plan attempted to combine tenements and street-grids with acknowledgement of the popular demand for privatised living space. Although Crown Street's first buildings were strongly influenced by current 'urban village' notions, more monumental designs were soon proposed. A master plan by Page & Park (1994) set out a range of unified designs. At its centre was Moffat Gardens – a 'garden square development' – incorporating a 'dialogue' between designs by Page & Park, Simister Monaghan, and a group by Elder & Cannon with twin towers designed to be seen in the round.

Does all of this add up to a Modernist revival? Evidence is growing, even within traditional building types such as schools. Lothian Regional Council's new Leith Academy (opened 1991; Laura Ross), was a 'street grid ... planned like a shopping centre'. Shopping centres themselves have become ever more Cumbernauld-like in their array of functions, which include post offices, nurseries, job centres and clinics. In an ironic twist at the new Gorbals, the shell of Thomson's Caledonia Road Church was rejected as the possible site for a new library in favour of a local supermarket location. Further, Modernist, open planning is again being considered in opposition to the hierarchical city grid. Could we yet arrive at a point where 1960s planning with its 'community' focus becomes a utopia in the face of the 'chaos' of 1990s individualistic consumerism?

The 1990s saw Scottish architecture at a point of apparent transition, not unlike the situation a century before, when the country seemed to be in the grip of a commercialism expressed through a bewildering eclecticism. Architecture, however, has continued to be identified with community rather than corporatism. This growing community focus has not produced an ostentatiously 'Scottish' architecture, but, in contrast, a self-consciously European one. The choice of a Spanish architect – Enric Miralles – to design Scotland's parliament has perhaps reinforced this outward-looking perspective.

Scottish architects' attempts to find the holy grail of Scottishness has kept architecture in a state of high anxiety for 500 years. There have been times when this search for a national style has been explicit, for example in the 19th and early 20th centuries. But beyond style there has been a remarkable continuity, which is most apparent in the use of stone. Whole cities – from the most ordinary tenement to the urban palaces of the super-rich – were built in finely dressed stone, even as the country was re-ordered by successive waves of modernisation.

Scotland has specialised, above all, in the true 'community' architecture of urbanism, where even the wealthiest were required to put 'city image' before self-image. This dynamic tension between the individual and the changing community has affected architectural output profoundly. Up until the very recent past, every dwelling, every factory, every shop, was conceived as part of a dignified but unpretentious whole. This was as true of small burghs like Dysart as it was of the world heritage city of Edinburgh. This output was achieved through a willing conformity to strict planning regulations which protected the 'built environment' from shoddy intrusions. But can this process continue? Are we prepared to see our demands for housing and leisure curtailed by design standards? In considering this question, we should remember that, unlike nature, our heritage is not disappearing, it is expanding. When we build, therefore, we should build well.

[Plate 1] Kelso Abbey, Borders (12th c.)

[Plate 2] Detail from Linlithgow Palace, West Lothian

Charles I, on his accession to the throne in 1625, immediately set about work on the palaces, but this was largely decorative. Murray's north quarter of Linlithgow was richly painted and decorated, with payments recorded for 'gilting and laying over with oyle collour the four orderis abone the utter yet'. The arms shown are those of James V on the outer gate: the Garter of England, the Thistle of Scotland, the Golden Fleece of Burgundy, and St Michael of France.

[Plate 3] South front of Stirling Palace block (from 1538)

With the palace block at Stirling, a startlingly new architecture was created. This new group dynamically built on the courtyard formula with a block containing two floors of lodgings and a basement floor, set on a raised site which turned the Forework into a terrace wall, almost anticipating the later conversion of European town walls to promenades. In effect, the palace block itself sits in (rather than forms) a courtyard, becoming a three-dimensional object. This new spatial condition, of course, allowed the palace block to 'interact' with the Great Hall, but also with the town itself. We are now beginning to see the use of 'set-piece' architecture, with buildings relating to one another and to the space they inhabit. The new block's façades were subtly articulated by a series of stepped wall-planes, with broad projections linked by arches containing statues, echoed by further small statues above the cornice. With its 'plesand sycht of all the four airthis', Stirling now seemed to address the town and the landscape, commanding the historically crucial battlefields of Stirling Bridge and Bannockburn. Internally, the new block was concerned with the comfort and pleasure of the monarch and his queen. The two lodgings had ceilings decorated with wooden roundels and stone fireplaces of explicitly French inspiration, one decorated with thistles.

[Plate 4] Sir James Hamilton of Finnart: Craignethan Castle, Lanarkshire (from c.1530)

[Plate 5]   Edzell Castle, Angus, from the north west

[Plate 6]   Edzell Castle, Angus, view from the garden originally created for Lord Edzell in 1604

[Plate 7]   Pinkie House, Musselburgh (1613), the long gallery undergoing restoration

[Plate 8]   Sir William Bruce: Loch Leven Castle, Fife (1679–93) from Kinross House

use, by Banff

began the three
his later designs:
to House and Duff
ult was a hunting
lge built (from
sterwork of 1740–2
) for the Duke of
e a feature to close
a or 'ride' at
Chatelherault also
he character of a
n sense of day
usiness of the great
g comprised an

elaborate screen wall linking two pairs
of tall pavilions, a composition of
highly theatrical character, but again
recalling Mar in its horizontality. In
1735–40, Adam became embroiled in
the most controversial of all his
designs: Duff House. Duff, whose
main block (but not its planned wings)
was built for Lord Braco, was an
unhappy commission that ended in
litigation. In this compact yet massive
block of four main storeys, Adam was
at last able to build a great house in
the form of a 'touer'. Braco objected to
the expensive extra storeys, but later
relented because, he said, 'the want of

it would spoill the Looks of such a
Monstrous house and indeed I wish
you and the house had been at the
Devil before it had begun'. Braco
was not a satisfied customer. He
wanted a compact dwelling, Adam
gave him a massive, Baroque house
weighed down with gigantic
pavilions on each corner. The pomp
of the exterior was matched inside by
the great open-plan staircase.
Because of the huge costs the interior
was never finished. The enraged
owner lowered his coach blinds every
time he passed the incomplete shell
of the building.

[Plate 10] Fort George (1748–69)
Designed by Colonel William Skinner,
built 1748–69 under the supervision of
successive members of the Adam
family, from William to James.

[Plate 11] Adelphi Terrace, London (1780s)

The first practical example of multi-level planning by the Adams was the Adelphi in London, where they speculatively built a large complex of terraced and flatted dwellings on a vaulted base. In 1771, Robert Adam also made an (unbuilt) design for a 'new town' at Bath, reached by a covered bridge with purpose-built shops.

[Plate 12] Alexander Nasmyth: Edinburgh from Princes Street with the Royal Institution under Construction, 1825

The picture presents a typical panoramic narrative of Edinburgh, with the latest ornament to the monumental city taking shape in the foreground. The Royal Institution (now the Royal Scottish Academy) was built and later extended (1822-6 and 1831-6) by W.H. Playfair for the Board of Manufactures and Fisheries with accommodation for other national bodies.

[Plate 13] Roger Morris: Inveraray Castle, built for the 3rd Duke of Argyll (from 1746), and Inveraray town

[Plate 14] John Michael Wright: 'Sir William Bruce' (1664)

[Plate 15] Unknown sculptor: 'William Adam' (1688–1748)

[Plate 16] Denis Dighton: 'George IV, Entrance into Edinburgh' (1822)

Scotland's position as a culturally autonomous nation within the world's most powerful state allowed her to project an independent national image which offered no threat to British interests. Scotland's 'new' image was all about the past. It was founded on the existing reputation of Ossian, and also the 'new Ossian', Sir Walter Scott. Architecture was important for Scott – as we can see in his organisation of the visit of King George IV to Edinburgh in 1822, when the city itself was laid out as a theatrical arena of living 'history'. Denis Dighton, the king's official painter, depicted the king's 'arrival' through the 'new entry' to the town created by Robert Adam over the bridge of Waterloo Place. Already, in 1788, Calton Hill had been used as a viewpoint for an Edinburgh 'panorama', but Scott's presentation was now as a city of history and of 'narrative', its architecture expressing its development over time. This is the beginning also of 'Old Town' romanticism, seen, at first, from a distance but soon to be penetrated and framed by 'improvements'. Already we can see Edinburgh holding a mirror up to itself, reflecting its romantic image.

In the foreground of Dighton's painting is Adam's Bridewell prison, still a symbol of the Enlightenment. On the 'hinge' of North Bridge–Princes Street is the same architect's Register House, a state building brought into play as a city monument and closing the uninterrupted view along the North and South Bridges, with their dramatic old/new interface. Clearly, Adam had laid the framework for an eclectic, set-piece city.

[Plate 17] Robert Adam:
No. 6 Charlotte Square, Edinburgh
(1791–1811)
*Completed after Adam's death, and
restored 1924–7 by the 4th Marquess
of Bute.*

[Plate 18]　No. 22 Park Circus, Glasgow (1872–4)

In the interior decoration of their villas, the mercantile class moved away from the classical richness visible at James Laurie's 52 Carlton Place (1802–4) towards a new eclecticism. In the houses of the very rich, all main rooms were now decorated at 'drawing-room level'. One of the most sumptuous examples was the house of iron manufacturer and exporter Walter MacFarlane, at 22 Park Circus, built by James Boucher. Externally, the house gave little away. Inside, it was a showroom of artistic cast iron, an art house presenting a procession of rooms of overwhelming opulence and craftsmanship, including an arcaded, domed ground-floor corridor, and an upper hall lit by a (patent) cast-iron dome (shown here as seen from below).

[Plate 19] Holmwood, Cathcart, Glasgow (1857–8)

In Thomson's interiors, the one 18th-century convention retained was the precise placing of furniture. No 'Victorian clutter' of clients' moveable contents was allowed. Thomson's showpiece interior was Holmwood, designed for the mill-owner James Couper – shown here undergoing restoration. The dining-room frieze reproduced Flaxman's illustrations of the Iliad, and the drawing-room had applied painted sections by Hugh Cameron. After Holmwood, Thomson's collaboration with the artist Daniel Cottier, marked a move away from vivid colour schemes to a new sensitivity.

[Plate 20]   Kingston Clinic, Edinburgh (1867–9)

Built as Craigend Park for the tailor William Christie by F.T. Pilkington, the design dramatically rejected dignified New Town classicism. From the 1850s, the residential spread of Edinburgh continued with boulevard and crescent developments of terraces, and areas of villas. For mid-19th century taste, the New Town pattern now seemed too austere. Once again, there began something of a flight from monumental city living to suburban villas. However an urban-suburban pattern was also continued in some new terraces of the Glasgow type, including the grandiosely Graeco-Italian section of Drumsheugh Gardens designed by Peddie & Kinnear (1874–8 [69]). The Glasgow model of Great Western Road was also picked up at Queensferry Road, with elevations by John Chesser, at Buckingham Terrace (from 1860) and Learmonth Terrace (from 1873).

[Plate 21]   David Bryce: Fettes College, Edinburgh (1864–70)

[Plate 22]   W. Atkinson with
Sir Walter Scott: Abbotsford, Borders
(1817–23)

[Plate 23]   Peddie & Kinnear: north
side of Cockburn Street, Edinburgh
(c.1859–64)

[Plate 24]   George Meikle Kemp:
the Scott Monument, Edinburgh
(1840–6)

142

[Plate 25]   Oscar Paterson: stained glass at No. 12 University Gardens, Glasgow (1900)

[Plate 26]   S. Henbest Capper & A.G. Sydney Mitchell (for Patrick Geddes): Ramsay Garden, Edinburgh (1892–4)

[Plate 27] Mount Stuart (from 1878)

John Patrick, 3rd Marquess of Bute, was the leading force behind the revival of worship and of conservation in 19th-century architecture. Bute was one of the world's richest men and, in common with many of his class, spent large amounts of money on buildings, largely of a romantic, neo-medieval cast. In the field of secular architecture, the strength of the classical tradition limited the impact of his medievalism to a few buildings of great individual importance. When Bute came to rebuild his own house, Mount Stuart, he commissioned Rowand Anderson, who drew on his own studies of secular medieval architecture in S. France and N. Italy. The result was very different from the fantasy-castles built for Bute in Wales by W. Burges: a rectangular palazzo block, with sheer, unbroken walls as at the contemporary Glasgow Central Station [82], and an eaves gallery and bellcast roof. Bute's intense mysticism was reflected in the astrological decoration of the interior, including the focal space of 'a vast hall, gleaming with light ... lined with rarest marbles, pavonazzetto, emperor's red, and pink-flushed alabaster'. At the same time, the house was fitted with the latest technology; it was the first in Scotland lit by electricity.

[Plate 28] Charles Rennie Mackintosh:
Daily Record Perspective (1901)

[Plate 29] Charles Rennie Mackintosh:
entrance to Hill House, Helensburgh (1902–4)

[Plate 30] Charles Rennie Mackintosh:
detail of Hill House (1902–4)

[Plate 31] Cornelius Armour: Luma
Lightbulb Factory, Glasgow (1936–8)
undergoing conversion into flats

[Plate 32]   Aerial view of the Empire Exhibition, Glasgow (1938) showing Scottish Avenue and the Scottish pavilions.

[Plate 33]   The Highland 'clachan' at the Empire Exhibition, Glasgow 1938

[Plate 36] **Dundee City Arts Centre (1998) – night-time computer image**
The new, more daringly expressed interface between the old and the new is typical of the work of Richard Murphy. His series of bold interventions set out to engage internal with external space, confronting new and old, inspired by a wide range of sources, including Geddes, Scarpa, De Stijl and European Vernacular. In 1992–3, he remodelled the Fruitmarket gallery in Edinburgh with an opened-up ground floor and a new 'industrial roofscape'. The concern with outlandish roofs was typical of a period of strict control of buildings' façades by planners, now chiefly concerned with 'urban design' issues. This type of flamboyant roof structure was thereafter employed on a diverse series of new build projects, including the Ibis Hotel, Edinburgh and Elder & Cannon's Brunswick Hotel (1996).

[Plate 37] **Elder & Cannon: Brunswick Hotel, Ingram Square, Glasgow (1996)**

[Plate 38] **Block of multi-storey flats being demolished at Ardler, Dundee (1996)**

[Plate 39] Benson & Forsyth: the
Museum of Scotland, Chambers
Street, Edinburgh (1995–8)

List of Illustrations

Colour Plates

Text Illustrations

[19] James Norie: 'Taymouth Castle' (1733); *courtesy of Antonia Reeve Photography/reproduced by permission of the Scottish National Portrait Gallery*

[20] Marcus Gheerverts the Younger: 'Alexander Seton' (1555–1622); *courtesy of Antonia Reeve Photography/reproduced by permission of the Scottish National Portrait Gallery*

[21] Tolquhon Castle, Tarves (rebuilt from 1584); *reproduced by permission of Historic Scotland*

[22] Huntly Castle, Aberdeenshire; *reproduced by permission of Historic Scotland*

[23] Craigievar, Aberdeenshire; *reproduced by permission of the Royal Commission on the Ancient and Historical Monuments of Scotland*

[24] Philabeg: plan and section of Craigievar Castle, Aberdeenshire; *reproduced by permission of the Royal Commission on the Ancient and Historical Monuments of Scotland*

[25] MacGibbon & Ross: Preston Tower, E. Lothian (16th century, raised in 17th century); *reproduced by permission of the Royal Commission on the Ancient and Historical Monuments of Scotland*

[26] Gordon of Rothiemay: map of Edinburgh (1647); *reproduced by permission of the Royal Commission on the Ancient and Historical Monuments of Scotland*

[27] Glasgow College (from 1630)

[28] Maybole Castle, Ayrshire (late 16th century)

[29] Argyll Lodging, Stirling (1632 and 1674); *reproduced by permission of Historic Scotland*

[30] Glasgow Tolbooth (1625–7)

[31] Holyrood Palace, Edinburgh (from 1670); from *Vitruvius Scoticus*

[32] MacGibbon & Ross: Thirlestane Castle, Lauder (rebuilt late 17th c., altered mid-19th c.); *reproduced by permission of Historic Scotland*

[33] Jacob de Witt, 'portrait of the 3rd Earl of Kinghorne'; *reproduced by permission of Strathmore Estates*

[34] Glamis Castle, interior; *reproduced by permission of the Royal Commission on the Ancient and Historical Monuments of Scotland*

[35] Plan of Holyrood Palace, Edinburgh; from *Vitruvius Scoticus*

[36] Sir William Bruce: Kinross House (1679–93); *reproduced by permission of the Royal Commission on the Ancient and Historical Monuments of Scotland*

[37] Sir William Bruce: central section of plan for Hopetoun House, near Edinburgh (1702); from *Vitruvius Scoticus*

[38] Earl of Mar: Stirling Castle, Stirling (1724); *reproduced by permission of Historic Scotland*

[39] William Adam & Earl of Mar: House of Dun, Angus (from 1730); *reproduced by permission of the Royal Commission on the Ancient and Historical Monuments of Scotland*

[40] William Adam: Mavisbank House, Midlothian (1723–6); *reproduced by permission of the Royal Commission on the Ancient and Historical Monuments of Scotland*

[41] William Adam: Edinburgh Royal Infirmary (1738–48); *reproduced by permission of the Royal Institute of Architects in Scotland*

[42] Robert Adam sketch of Fort George; *reproduced by permission of Keith Adam*

[43] Sir William Bruce: Stirling Tolbooth (1703–4); *reproduced by permission of the Royal Commission on the Ancient and Historical Monuments of Scotland*

[44] James Craig's plan of Edinburgh New Town (1767); *reproduced by permission of the Royal Commission on the Ancient and Historical Monuments of Scotland*

[45] Robert Adam: north side of Charlotte Square, Edinburgh (from 1792, square completed 1820); *reproduced by permission of the Royal Commission on the Ancient and Historical Monuments of Scotland*

[46] Robert Adam: plan for South Bridge, Edinburgh (1785); *reproduced by permission of the Trustees of Sir John Soane's Museum*

[47] Tron Kirk, Edinburgh (1633, altered 1785–7, steeple 1828); *reproduced by permission of the Royal Commission on the Ancient and Historical Monuments of Scotland*

[48] Robert Adam: elevation for Edinburgh University (1789)

[49] Robert Adam: plan for Bridewell prison (1791–5); *reproduced by permission of the Royal Commission on the Ancient and Historical Monuments of Scotland*

[50] James Tassie: 'Robert Adam' (c.1773); *reproduced by permission of the Scottish National Portrait Gallery*

[51] Robert Adam: Gosford House, E. Lothian (1790–1803), later altered; *reproduced by permission of the Royal Commission on the Ancient and Historical Monuments of Scotland*

[52] Robert Adam: view of Cluny Castle; *reproduced by permission of the Trustees of Sir John Soane's Museum*

[53] Culzean Castle, Ayrshire (1777–92)

[54] Daniel Robertson: design for a gate lodge (c.1800); *reproduced by permission of Keith Adam*

[55] Port Dundas Canal Offices, Glasgow (1812); *photograph by Colin McPherson*

[56] John Miller: main entrance to Melrose Station (1847–9); *photograph by Colin McPherson*

[57] Aerial view of Woodlands Hill, Glasgow; *reproduced by permission of the Royal Commission on the Ancient and Historical Monuments of Scotland*

[58] William Stark: Justiciary Court, Saltmarket, Glasgow (1809–14) later remodelled; *reproduced by permission of the Royal Commission on the Ancient and Historical Monuments of Scotland*

[59] William Playfair: St Stephen's Church, Edinburgh (1827–8); *reproduced by permission of the Royal Commission on the Ancient and Historical Monuments of Scotland*

[60] Calton Hill with Thomas Hamilton's Old Royal High School, Edinburgh (1825–9); *photograph by Colin McPherson*

[61] James Milne: St Bernard's Crescent, Edinburgh (from 1824); *photograph by Colin McPherson*

[62] Aerial view of the north-western New Town, Edinburgh (from 1820s); *reproduced by permission of the Royal Commission on the Ancient and Historical Monuments of Scotland*

[63] Castle Street, Aberdeen; *reproduced by permission of Aberdeen City Council*

[64] Archibald Simpson (1790–1847); *reproduced by permission of the Royal Institute of Architects in Scotland*

[65] The Necropolis, Glasgow (from 1833); *photograph by Colin McPherson*

[66] Charles Wilson: Free Church College, Glasgow (1856–61)

[67] Charles Wilson: unbuilt design for Kelvinside Parish Church, Glasgow (1858); *reproduced by permission of the Royal Commission on the Ancient and Historical Monuments of Scotland*

[68] Alexander Thomson: St Vincent Street Church, Glasgow (1857–9); *reproduced by permission of the Royal Commission on the Ancient and Historical Monuments of Scotland*

[69] Peddie & Kinnear: Drumsheugh Gardens, Edinburgh (1874); *photograph by Colin McPherson*

[70] Alexander Thomson: Walmer Crescent, Glasgow (1857–62); *reproduced by permission of the Royal Commission on the Ancient and Historical Monuments of Scotland*

[71] Alexander Thomson: Egyptian Halls, Union Street, Glasgow (1871–3); *Royal Commission on the Ancient and Historical Monuments of Scotland*

[72] David Hamilton: Hamilton Palace new façade (from 1822); *reproduced by permission of the Royal Commission on the Ancient and Historical Monuments of Scotland*

[73] Villa, Pollokshields, Glasgow (later 19th c.)

[74] W.H. Playfair: Donaldson's Hospital, Edinburgh (1841–51)

[75] Peddie & Kinnear: Aberdeen Town House (1866–74); *reproduced by permission of the Royal Commission on the Ancient and Historical Monuments of Scotland*

[76] Abbotsford, Borders, The servants' entrance (1817–23); *photograph by Colin McPherson*

[77] Sir George Gilbert Scott: St Mary's Cathedral, Edinburgh (1874–1917); *reproduced by permission of the Royal Commission on the Ancient and Historical Monuments of Scotland*

[78] George Gilbert Scott: Glasgow University (1864–70)

[79] David Bryce: British Linen Bank (now Bank of Scotland), Edinburgh (1846–51); *photograph by Colin McPherson*

[80] James Gowans (1821–90); *reproduced by permission of the Royal Commission on the Ancient and Historical Monuments of Scotland*

[81] James Gowans: 'Rockville', Edinburgh (1858); *reproduced by permission of the Royal Commission on the Ancient and Historical Monuments of Scotland*

[82] Rowand Anderson: Central Station Hotel, Glasgow (1882–4), extended by James Miller (1900–8); *reproduced by permission of the Royal Commission on the Ancient and Historical Monuments of Scotland*

[83] James Miller: No. 8 (1904) and No. 10 (c.1900) Lowther Terrace; A.G. Sydney Mitchell: No. 9 Lowther Terrace (1904–6) – Glasgow; *reproduced by permission of the Royal Commission on the Ancient and Historical Monuments of Scotland*

[84] William Forbes Skene: Cluny Castle, Aberdeenshire (late 16th c.); *from MacGibbon and Ross*

[85] James Thomson: Connal Building, West George Street, Glasgow (1898–1900); *reproduced by permission of the Royal Commission on the Ancient and Historical Monuments of Scotland*

[86] Sir John Fowler & Sir Benjamin Baker: Forth Bridge (1882–90); *reproduced by permission of the Royal Commission on the Ancient and Historical Monuments of Scotland*

[87] Rowand Anderson: 'Allermuir', Colinton, Edinburgh (1879); *reproduced by permission of the Royal Commission on the Ancient and Historical Monuments of Scotland*

[88] Charles Rennie Mackintosh: Scotland Street School, Glasgow (1902–6); *reproduced by permission of the Royal Commission on the Ancient and Historical Monuments of Scotland*

[89] William Young: City Chambers, Glasgow (1883–8); *reproduced by permission of the Royal Commission on the Ancient and Historical Monuments of Scotland*

[90] Fine Arts Pavilion, Glasgow Exhibition (1911)

[91] Patrick Geddes (1865–1932)

[92] J.J. Burnet: St Molio's Church, Arran (1886)

[93] Robert Lorimer: Thistle Chapel, annexe to St Giles, Edinburgh (1909–11); *reproduced by permission of the Royal Commission on the Ancient and Historical Monuments of Scotland*

[94] John Patrick, 3rd Marquess of Bute (1847–1902): *reproduced by permission of the Mount Stuart Trust*

[95] Rowand Anderson: Scottish National Portrait Gallery, Edinburgh (1884–9); *reproduced by permission of the National Galleries of Scotland*

[96] Marischal College, Aberdeen (1893–8); *Royal Commission on the Ancient and Historical Monuments of Scotland*

[97] F.H. Newbery: 'Charles Rennie Mackintosh' (1914); *Scottish National Portrait Gallery (National Galleries of Scotland)*

[98] Charles Rennie Mackintosh: interior of Hill House, Helensburgh; (1902–4); *Royal Commission on the Ancient and Historical Monuments of Scotland*

[99] Charles Rennie Mackintosh: House for an Art Lover, Glasgow (1901)

[100 & 101] Charles Rennie Mackintosh: Glasgow School of Art (1905–9); *101 reproduced by permission of the Royal Commission on the Ancient and Historical Monuments of Scotland*

[102] James Sellars: Mitchell Theatre, Glasgow (1873–7); *photograph by Colin McPherson*

[103] Burnet & Campbell: Athenaeum Theatre, Buchanan Street, Glasgow (1891); *Royal Commission on the Ancient and Historical Monuments of Scotland*

[104] J.J. Burnet: Atlantic Chambers, Argyle Street, Glasgow (1899–1900); *reproduced by permission of the Royal Commission on the Ancient and Historical Monuments of Scotland*

[105] Salmon & Gillespie: Lion Chambers, Hope Street, Glasgow (1904–7); *reproduced by permission of the Royal Commission on the Ancient and Historical Monuments of Scotland*

[106] J.J. Burnet: Alhambra Theatre, Glasgow (1911); *reproduced by permission of the Royal Commission on the Ancient and Historical Monuments of Scotland*

[107] Robert Lorimer: building the Scottish National War Memorial (1924–7); *reproduced by permission of Dr P.D. Savage*

[108] H. & D. Barclay: Jordanhill College, Glasgow (1913–22); *courtesy of Ranald MacInnes*

[109] J.A. Carfrae: Tollcross School, Edinburgh (1911–13); *Royal Commission on the Ancient and Historical Monuments of Scotland*

[110] Thomas Tait: St Andrew's House, Edinburgh (1936–9); *reproduced by permission of Historic Scotland*

[111] 'Empirex', Glasgow (1938)

[112] 'Louisville House, No.4 Louisville Avenue, Aberdeen (1975); *Aberdeen City Council*

[113] Bungalow development at Morningside Gardens, Edinburgh (early 20th-c.); *Aberdeen City Council*

[114] Ian Lindsay (1906–66)

[115] Cruachan Dam hydro-electric scheme (1960–5)

[116] Patrick Geddes: Valley Section

[117] Reiach & Hurd: 'Building Scotland' (1941)

[118] Robert Matthew: Turnhouse Airport, Edinburgh (1954–6); *reproduced by permission of the Royal Commission on the Ancient and Historical Monuments of Scotland*

[119] Aerial view of Hutchesontown Gorbals, Glasgow (1956); *reproduced by permission of the Royal Commission on the Ancient and Historical Monuments of Scotland*

[120] Peter Womersley: Port Murray, Maidens (1960–3)

[121] Geoffrey Copcutt: Cumbernauld Town Centre (1963–7); *reproduced by permission of the Royal Commission on the Ancient and Historical Monuments of Scotland*

[122] Gillespie, Kidd & Coia: St Peter's Seminary, Cardross (1959–66); *Royal Commission on the Ancient and Historical Monuments of Scotland*

[123] Basil Spence: Area 'C'. Hutchesontown Town, Glasgow (1960–6); *reproduced by permission of the Royal Institute of Architects in Scotland*

[124] Benson & Forsyth: Maiden Lane, London (1976–81); *courtesy of Richard Crotch*

[125] St Paul's Church, Glenrothes (1956–7); *courtesy of J. Roman Rock*

[126] John Richards (RMJM): University of Stirling (1966–73); *reproduced by permission of the Royal Commission on the Ancient and Historical Monuments of Scotland*

[127] Provost Ross's House, Aberdeen in 1950; *Aberdeen City Council*

[128] Provost Ross's House, Aberdeen, after restoration (1978); *reproduced by permission of the City of Aberdeen Council*

[129] Johnston & Groves-Raines: Landmark Visitor Centre, Stirling (1971)

[130] Terry Farrell: Edinburgh International Conference Centre (1993–5); *photograph by Harvey Wood*

[131] Gillespie, Kidd & Coia: Robinson College, Cambridge (1977–80); *reproduced by permission of the Royal Commission on the Ancient and Historical Monuments of Scotland*

[132] Page & Park: the Italian Centre, Glasgow (1988–94) with City Chambers in the background; *reproduced by permission of the Royal Commission on the Ancient and Historical Monuments of Scotland*

[133] Scott & Wilson, Kirkpatrick & Partners: frontispiece from Report on a Highway Plan for Glasgow (1965); *reproduced by permission of the City of Glasgow*

[134] J. Swan: Glasgow Infirmary (c.1829)

[135] Ian Begg: St Mungo Museum, Glasgow (1990–3); *photograph by Colin McPherson*

[136] D.G. Bannerman, Lanark County Buildings, Hamilton (1959–4); *reproduced by permission of the Royal Commission on the Ancient and Historical Monuments of Scotland*

Further Reading

N. Allen (ed.), *Scottish Pioneers of the Greek Revival*, 1984

Architectural Heritage 3, 1992 (J. Lowrey [ed.], *The Age of Mackintosh*)

G. Beard, *The Work of Robert Adam*, 1978

R.W. Billings, *The Baronial and Ecclesiastical Antiquities of Scotland*, 4 volumes, 1845–52

A. Bolton, *The Architecture of Robert and James Adam*, 2 volumes, 1922

D. Brett, *Charles Rennie Mackintosh*, 1992

I. Campbell, 'A Romanesque Revival and the Early Renaissance in Scotland', *Journal of the Society of Architectural Historians*, September 1995

R. Crampsey, *The Empire Exhibition of 1938*, 1988

K. Cruft and A. Fraser (eds), *James Craig*, 1995

M. Davis, *The Castles and Mansions of Ayrshire*, 1991

R. Dixon and S. Muthesius, *Victorian Architecture*, 1978

A. Drexler (ed.), *The Architecture of the Ecole des Beaux-Arts*, 1977

B. Edwards, *Basil Spence 1907–1976*, 1995

J.G. Dunbar *The Architecture of Scotland*, 1978

R. Fawcett, *Edinburgh Castle*, 1986

— *Scottish Architecture from the Accession of the Stewarts to the Reformation*, 1994

J. Fleming, *Robert Adam and his Circle*, 1962

J. Gifford, *William Adam*, 1989

M. Glendinning and S. Muthesius, *Tower Block: Modern Public Housing in England, Scotland, Wales and Northern Ireland*, 1994

M. Glendinning, R. MacInnes, Aonghus MacKechnie, *A History of Scottish Architecture from the Renaissance to the Present Day*, 1996

A. Gomme, D.M. Walker, *Architecture of Glasgow*, 1968

I.R. Gow, *The Scottish Interior*, 1992

I.R. Gow and A. Rowan (eds), *Scottish Country Houses*, 1995

G. Hay, *The Architecture of Scottish Post-Reformation Churches*, 1957

H-R. Hitchcock, *Architecture: Nineteenth and Twentieth Centuries*, 1958

D. Howard, *Scottish Architecture, Reformation to Restoration*, 1995

P. & J. Kinchin, *Glasgow's Great Exhibitions*, 1988

D. King, *The Complete Works of Robert and James Adam*, 1991

B. Little, *The Life and Work of James Gibbs*, 1955

M. Lynch, *Scotland: a New History*, 1991

D. McAra, *Sir James Gowans*, 1975

J. Macaulay, *The Gothic Revival 1745–1845*, 1975

— *The Classical Country House in Scotland*, 1987

— *Hill House*, 1994

R. McFadzean, *The Life and Work of Alexander Thomson*, 1979

D. MacGibbon and T. Ross, *The Castellated and Domestic Architecture of Scotland*, 5 volumes, 1887–1892

The Ecclesiastical Architecture of Scotland, 3 volumes, 1896–7

C. McKean, *The Scottish Thirties*, 1987

— 'The Scottishness of Scottish Architecture', in P.H. Scott (ed.), *Scotland: A Concise Cultural History*, 1993

S. McKinstry, *Rowand Anderson*, 1991

R. Macleod, *Charles Rennie Mackintosh*, 1968

Macmillan Encyclopedia of Architects, New York, 1982

D. Mays, 'A Profile of Sir George Washington Browne', *Architectural Heritage 3*, 1992

H. Meller, *Patrick Geddes*, 1990

I. Rae, *Charles Cameron*, 1971

P. Reed, *Glasgow: The Forming of a City*, 1993

A. Reiach and R. Hurd, *Building Scotland*, 1941/1944

P. Robertson (ed.), *Charles Rennie Mackintosh – The Architectural Papers*, 1990

R.W.K. Rogerson, *Jack Coia*, 1986

A. Rowan, 'The Building of Hopetoun', *Architectural History* 27, 1984

Royal Institute of British Architects, *James MacLaren*, 1990

P. Savage, *Lorimer and the Edinburgh Craft Designers*, 1980

Scottish Arts Council, *Sir William Bruce*, 1970 (introduction by J.G. Dunbar)

G. Stamp and S. McKinstry (eds), *Greek Thomson*, 1994

I.C. Tabraham and D. Grove, *Fortress Scotland and the Jacobites*, 1995

A.A. Tait, *The Landscape Garden in Scotland*, 1980

— *Robert Adam: Drawings and Imagination*, 1993

Vitruvius Scoticus, c.1812 (reprint, ed. J. Simpson, 1980)

D.M. Watters, 'David Hamilton's Lennox Castle', *Architectural Heritage*, 1995

P. Willis, *New Architecture in Scotland*, 1977

F. Worsdall, *The Glasgow Tenement*, 1989

A.J. Youngson, *The Making of Classical Edinburgh*, 1975

See also the *Buildings of Scotland* series, and the RIAS illustrated architectural guides, both of which deal with individual cities and counties.

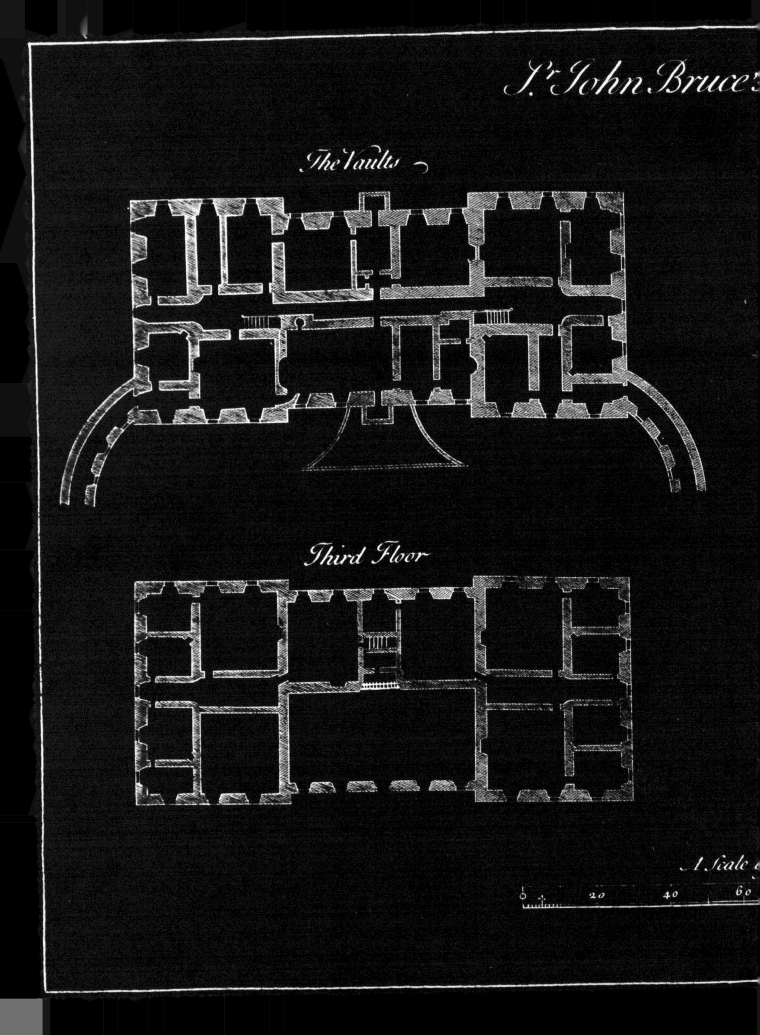

Sr John Bruce's

The Vaults

Third Floor

A Scale

0   20   40   60